# Crash Course: To Recovery and Beyond

JASON A. PLOTKIN, ESQ.

ISBN: 978-1-7330190-2-6

# DEDICATION

This book is dedicated to the late Edward Pinder, a mentor and beacon whose influence reached far beyond his role as a respected attorney. Ed's life was a remarkable blend of hard work, compassion, and steadfast dedication, not only to his legal profession and community as a cherished softball coach, but also to his family, whom he loved and prioritized with deep devotion. More than a lawyer, Ed was a role model, a friend, a source of joy and laughter in challenging times, and a family man who demonstrated the balance of professional success with personal warmth and care. His unique ability to connect with people, whether in professional attire or on the sports field, left an unforgettable impact on all who knew him, including Jason Plotkin, who continues Ed's legacy of integrity, hard work, and community engagement. This book pays tribute to Ed Pinder's extraordinary life, a life that exemplified the true impact of kindness, strong character, and how profoundly one individual can touch the lives of many, in both public and private realms.

# Following Jason's Lead: Colleagues Share Their Mentorship Experiences

---

## **Guiding with Integrity:** How Jason Shapes Our Firm's Future

As the practice manager at Jason's law firm, I have had the privilege of witnessing firsthand the profound impact of his journey, eloquently captured in "Crash Course." This book isn't just a recounting of harrowing experiences; it's a profound narrative that encapsulates the essence of resilience, empathy, and transformative growth.

Being mentored by Jason has been an enlightening experience. His deep care for his clients and the passion with which he represents them stem from his own personal battles with adversity. This unique perspective has brought an invaluable dimension to our practice. Jason doesn't just see a case; he sees the person behind it, their struggles, fears, and hopes. This human-centric approach has been a guiding light in our firm, reshaping the way we approach our work.

"Crash Course" is more than Jason's story. It's a testament to the power of empathy in the legal profession. His narrative goes beyond the legalities of personal injury law, delving into the emotional and psychological impact of such events on individuals. As readers, we are not only drawn into the depth of his personal struggles but are also given a front-row seat to the evolution of an attorney who uses his experiences to champion the cause of his clients.

What truly sets this book apart is the sincerity and vulnerability with which Jason shares his story. It's rare to find a legal professional who is willing to open up about their personal trials in such a public manner. This honesty resonates throughout the firm, creating a culture of openness and genuine concern for our clients.

In summary, "Crash Course" is a compelling read, not just for those in the legal field but for anyone who appreciates a story of overcoming adversity and using those experiences to make a positive impact in the lives of others. Jason's story is a powerful reminder of the human element in the practice of law and the incredible difference empathy can make in the pursuit of justice. –**Charlotte Lescallett**, Practice Manager at the Pinder Plotkin Legal Team

---

**In the Trenches:** How Jason's Strategies Resonate in Litigation

As the Litigation Partner at Jason's law firm, reading "Crash Course" has been an invigorating experience. This book is more than a personal narrative; it's a testament to Jason's unyielding resilience and deep empathy, qualities that he has instilled in every aspect of our firm's litigation approach.

Being mentored by Jason, who fought so valiantly through his own challenges, has profoundly influenced our firm's philosophy. His journey through the aftermath of two devastating car accidents, battling with insurance companies and the legal system, exemplifies a fighter's spirit. This same spirit is what we bring to the courtroom for our clients. Jason's personal battles have become a blueprint for our aggressive litigation strategy, combining tenacity with a deep understanding of our clients' struggles.

Jason's empathy, born from his personal experiences, has been transformative. It's one thing to understand a client's case; it's another to feel the depth of their trauma and fight for them as if it were your own battle. This empathetic aggression is what sets our litigation approach apart. We don't just represent our clients; we fight for them with a personal investment and intensity inspired by Jason's own resilience.

"Crash Course" is a compelling reflection of how personal adversity can forge professional excellence. Jason's story has not just shaped our firm's culture; it has revolutionized our approach to litigation. We fight hard in the courtroom, mirroring the way Jason fought for his recovery and rights. This book is a powerful reminder of the strength that can be born from hardship and the impact of a deeply personal commitment to advocacy.

For anyone who has suffered the impact of a car accident, or knows someone who has, this book offers more than legal insights; it offers a sense of solidarity and hope, affirming that from even the most challenging experiences, strength and understanding can emerge. It highlights our firm's commitment to fighting tirelessly for our clients, fueled by the same determination and empathy that Jason showed in overcoming his own trials. – **Tony Balsamo**, Litigation Partner at The Pinder Plotkin Legal Team

## Voices of Trust: Unveiling Jason's Journey through Client Testimonials

In the forward of this book, we delve into the personal journey of Jason, a testament to the empathy and advocacy he extends to each of his clients. His experiences not only shape his professional approach but also resonate deeply with those he serves, fostering a unique connection that goes beyond mere representation. This is vividly reflected in the over 300 five-star reviews from clients, a compelling endorsement of his commitment to excellence. Below, you will find a selection of these reviews, each telling a story of trust, satisfaction, and profound impact, illuminating the difference Jason has made in the lives of so many.

If only I could rate this place more than five stars I would. They've been more than patient, understanding and supportive extremely welcoming. I've worked with them for 7 years. I wouldn't choose any other firm to work with. 10/10 would have to recommend to anyone who needs legal assistance! - Debbie L.☆☆☆☆☆

The Pinder Plotkin team is the team to go with. They take care of all your needs very patient and answers every question no matter how many times you ask it. Even with not knowing how things would go they took the worry and fear and made it such a positive experience. I'm a FOREVER CLIENT. - Tangi S.☆☆☆☆☆

Navigating through any legal issues is tough, but Jason and Charlotte will ease your stress and really help you understand the process you are going through. From day one, they took my case seriously, and reassured me every step of the way. They will fight for you and in my opinion go above and beyond to get the best possible outcome for you. Thank you, Jason and Charlotte, words could never express how grateful I am for you. - Elizabeth N.☆☆☆☆☆

Thank you, Pinder Plotkin Legal team, for settling my auto accident case. Your team was pleasant to work with and I am happy with the settlement amount. My only regret is that I did not contact your office sooner after my accident. I feel like I was being jerked around and taken advantage of by the insurance companies until the Pinder Plotkin Legal team got involved in the case. I would recommend them to anyone that was in an auto accident. - Ruth B. ☆☆☆☆☆

When I have reached out to the Pinder Plotkin team, they worked hard to assist me my legal matter. Everyone is patient and kind and explained everything to me that I did not understand in such a way that made sense to me and did not go over my head! I would highly recommend this team to anyone who needs legal assistance!!! I would give them 10 stars if it would let me!! Thanks again for all the info and help!!! - Joe S.☆☆☆☆☆

Very satisfied with the Pinder Plotkin Legal team! I worked with the Parkville office. Nancy and Charlotte were very Informative and pleasant throughout the entire process. If I didn't understand something they would take the time to explain in detail to answer all my questions and concerns. My phone calls from them were prompt also. Tony and Jason were great to work with also explaining the entire process and working very hard on my case. I would rate them a Five Star Review!!! Thank you all for your time and effort with my case!!! - Mary & Bob S.☆☆☆☆☆

Exceptional Legal Advocacy - 5 Stars for Pinder Plotkin! I can't speak highly enough about the outstanding legal services provided by Pinder Plotkin. From the moment I engaged with their team, it was clear that I was in the hands

of dedicated professionals. The attorneys at Pinder Plotkin are not only experts in their field but also compassionate advocates who genuinely care about their clients. They took the time to understand my unique situation and provided clear guidance throughout the entire process. Pinder Plotkin's attention to detail and strategic approach were instrumental in achieving a positive outcome for my legal matter. I highly recommend Pinder Plotkin to anyone seeking top-notch legal representation. They are the best in the business. Thank you, Pinder Plotkin, for your exceptional service!
- Tiffany G. ☆☆☆☆☆

I been a client since 2017 and I had a good experience with them as far as getting results and being treated like family, I had a major injury and the whole team was very supportive and stayed on top of my case, I was able to maintain my bills due to being out of work for a year and they made it possible for me and I appreciate the settlement I received in which it helped me with starting my own businesses. I just retained them again, so I look forward to starting this process again. They are the best. - Camron A. ☆☆☆☆☆

I found Pinder Plotkin to be very helpful with my issue. I reached out to their office via a link I saw, and they reached out to me quickly. The gentleman I spoke with was very knowledgeable, compassionate, and willing to assist me with the car accident I had. I felt that he listened to what my concerns were. From what he heard and advised me, I no longer felt my issue was hopeless. I felt confident I was in capable hands. Thank you! - Delta M. ☆☆☆☆☆

I heard back from a representative of their office almost immediately after I submitted a request for a consultation. My conversation with Jason was very informative and extremely helpful! Jason was very knowledgeable, and he was able to give me a lot of valuable information on how we should proceed with our case moving forward. I definitely feel less anxious about our situation now that I have a better understanding of it, in addition to the legal assistance of a knowledgeable professional. - Kimberly T. ☆☆☆☆☆

WHEN I SAY THAT WHEN YOU ARE IN NEED OF AN ATTORNEY IN AN ACCIDENT CALL PINDER PLOTKIN! Don't HESITATE! CALL THEM! Professionalism is an Understatement! CHARLOTTE FANTASTIC CARING WOMAN! JASON! You already know you are PERFECTION. - Shaquita M. ☆☆☆☆☆

Jason and Charlotte are wonderful to work with. Made the process very smooth and easy to go through. Highly recommend their legal team! Jason and Charlotte are wonderful to work with. Made the process very smooth and easy to go through. Highly recommend their legal team! The Pinder Plotkin team is fantastic. Just a few adjectives... responsive, honest, caring, thorough, personable, professional. I highly recommend Mr. Plotkin and the team for, quite simply, just a call to see what they think about your respective issue. It's refreshing to realize, quickly, they honestly care about your health and wellbeing, yet they are transparent, straight shooters, so to speak. There's often a fine line in play, and Mr. Plotkin is clear and concise in communicating expectations. The Pinder Plotkin team has your best interests in focus, offering a sense of security when life's unexpected cards are dealt. Give them a call and you'll feel like you made the right decision the moment you hang up and take that much-needed exhale. - Sierra F. ☆☆☆☆☆

Jason, Charlotte, and Tony were absolutely amazing! I was in a car accident 4 years ago, they made sure I was taken care of and even though we had a lot of setbacks due to Covid, they never made me feel like my case (or me) were not important. Tony knew my medical history better than I did!

The whole team worked so hard for me the last 4 years and didn't get annoyed with any of my phone calls (I called them a lot lol). I have already been suggesting them to friends that need lawyers and will definitely get their services again if I ever need them! - The R. ☆☆☆☆☆

After months of stress, my daughter was referred to Pinder and Plotkin to take charge of her workers compensation case. Shannon, from the start, put her at ease and assured her Pinder and Plotkin was there to relieve her of the stressful process, allowing her to concentrate on healing. In addition, there is no question too large or small, and both Shannon and Jason explain in a way that is understandable! - Judy C ☆☆☆☆☆

Since I met the incredible Pinder Plotkin, they were amazing. They listen to every problem detail by detail and to making sure I received the best resolution possible. After my incident I felt lost and didn't know what to do I was physically and mentally drained and I was brushed off by my car insurance. Pinder Plotkin helps me get the right treatment into getting me back on my feet. Their response was always on time, and they make sure to obtain everything needed in order to give me the help I deserved. SPECIAL THANKS TO JASON PLOTKIN, NANCY ELLIS, AND TONY BALSAMO for giving me justice and for always having great customer services every time we spoke. You guys are amazing, and I will surely be recommending you to every single person who needed help like me. You made it possible thank you so much. - Desere J. ☆☆☆☆☆

I have to say if I could let anyone know how I feel about this business is that they go above and beyond to help me. There always there when I contact them for help. I honestly don't know how to thank them enough for what they have continued to do for me. If you want someone that will get you the help that you need and know that they have the best interest for you then I would recommend them as one of the best. I was recommended by someone also that have used them, and they were 100% right that this lawyer and his team will help you so you can sit back and not stress. If there was a rate 1-10, I would say 10. Thank you for all your help, guys. - Joseph S. ☆☆☆☆☆

Mr. Jason Plotkin and his team were a beacon of HOPE to my family and I as we navigated through a difficult time. Prior to meeting with Mr. Plotkin, we had gone through a series of nightmare while working with another lawyer's office. Pinder Plotkin came in highly recommended, and we were willing to take the leap of FAITH. When you talk about excellent communication and world class client relationship, this is your ONE STOP SHOP. In our first consultation we were reassured of the steps that would be taken to achieve a satisfactory resolution. Mr. Jason Plotkin and his legal assistant Ms. Nancy are the dynamic duo. You can always expect to get the latest update on what is happening with your case and the likely next steps. During the instances where we had to be represented, Mr. Jason defended us in the highest regard. My family and I are eternally grateful for your stellar service and hereby unreservedly recommend Jason Plotkin and the entire Pinder Plotkin Legal Team for a world class experience. We received a favorable outcome, and it would not have been possible without the skills, competencies, experience, effective communication and collaboration from the Pinder Plotkin Team. Thank You! Thank You! Thank You! - Kondi S. ☆☆☆☆☆

I am not even a client yet~ but I hope that I will be soon! I was treated with the utmost of respect. All of my questions were addressed. Care and compassion for me as a human being have happened with every single person/point of contact that I have had with the Pinder Plotkin team. I have had some issues with other attorneys ~ night and day

difference! And ethics ~ I was even referred back to someone because they don't steal business from other people. WOW. I am beyond appreciative and impressed. Give them a call!
- Aileen G. ☆☆☆☆☆

I greatly appreciated the humanity perspective provided by my attorney, Jason Plotkin. He listened to me and showed genuine care and concern toward me during this traumatic experience, for that I will be forever grateful. The office staff were very professional and timely in their correspondence, specifically the paralegal assigned (Nancy). Thank you all for an awesome experience!
- Janitha M. ☆☆☆☆☆

This legal team is awesome! The stay engaged from beginning to end. My [claim] opened in 2017 and closed in 2021. I would totally forget about the case for months, but the never failed to contact me with updates and to ask if I had any questions. When I thought it was a list cause the team would never give up. They were always polite and positive; I could hear them smile over the phone. They felt my pain and were always very patient took all the time with me that I needed. I would highly recommend this Team to anyone! - Annette B. ☆☆☆☆☆

The Pinder Plotkin Legal Team is a group of lawyers and paralegals who are friendly, respectful and easy to talk to about your concerns. It seems to me that their priority is to provide you with the best professional legal representation with as minimal stress as possible. It has been my experience that lawyers can stress you out or calm you down. They will give you confidence and put your mind as ease that you have the best representation available. - Richard S. ☆☆☆☆☆

Pinder Plotkin law firm is an honest, professional, caring team of individuals who work hard for every client. We

have worked with them as referral partners in our chiropractic office for several years now and we are proud to send our patients there and care for their clients. The level of service and attentiveness they give is lost on most business moguls. These people care about people not just the money they are making. It is unusual to find this kind of lawyer in a big city these days. We highly recommend them!!
- Melody L.☆☆☆☆☆

I have worked specifically with Jason Plotkin on multiple occasions. Each time he was very responsive to my calls and provided sound legal advice and representation. He is courteous and treats you like family. I would recommend using Jason Plotkin for any legal services.
- Tammy L.☆☆☆☆☆

My family and myself have had the pleasure of working with the Pinder Plotkin legal team many times. Estates, Workers Comp, Student loan issues, Auto accidents. They are fully staffed to handle all your legal needs. This firm is caring and treat you with the utmost respect. I cannot thank them for all the help they have given me and my family. Jason Plotkin and Charlotte and staff thank you for always being there for us. - Chrisann R. ☆☆☆☆☆

An excellent job performed by an excellent firm. The Pinder Plotkin Legal team took over my personal injury case from another law firm, and right away I could see a drastic difference in organization, record collecting and communication. I cannot recommend them enough.
- Rob W. ☆☆☆☆☆

I highly recommend the Pinder Plotkin Legal Team, Jason and his staff are always professional, but also provide sincere empathy for your issue(s) that you are experiencing and require legal assistance. In most circumstances where seeking an attorney for guidance and representation can be very scary and difficult, this team will put you ~~at ease and~~ ☆☆☆☆☆ will rest a sure you are in good hands! - Dawn M.

I've been dealing with this law firm for almost 3 years Jason is the best attorney I've ever come across he makes it as less stressful as possible Jason and his staff Charlotte is wonderful as well, she is very caring and understanding y'all would be a fool not to hire Jason. - Shannon D. ☆☆☆☆☆

The integrity driven practice of The Pinder Plotkin Legal Team had my best intentions front and center every time I met with them. From my first call to the office all the way up to my hearing, they went above and beyond to help me with my case. I felt cared for and informed the whole way through the process. No cheesy commercials, just experience and results from this law firm. I wish I could give them 10 STARS! Thank you so much Pinder Plotkin Legal Team.
- Ken F. ☆☆☆☆☆

With this being my first time going through this situation, I was very nervous. After speaking with Jason, my nerves settled a little, since he walked me through the process and was able to answer all of my questions and concerns to my satisfaction. The day being in court, he was able to calm my nerves completely. I am very thankful for the help, knowledge and professionalism that he provided and how friendly the firm has been with us. I would highly recommend Jason and his team to anyone! - Thomas A. ☆☆☆☆☆

Worked with Jason, very professional who did everything he promised and more! Everyone I had interactions with was very helpful and treated me as part of the family. Highly recommend, especially like how he shared and discussed every outcome possible, and not just the one I was hoping for. Would definitely use again.

- Chris K. ☆☆☆☆☆

From My Story to Yours: **Share Your Experience**

As we turn the page to my story, remember that each journey is unique, including yours. I invite you to not only delve into the chapters of my experiences but also to share your own. Your story matters, and I would be honored to hear it. Connect with me and let your voice be heard –

**https://www.pinderplotkin.com/crash-course**

Additionally, for a more personal touch, you can watch my story unfold – simply scan the QR code provided below. Your narratives and experiences are invaluable, and together, they weave a tapestry of resilience and learning. Share your story, join the conversation, and become a part of this ever-growing community.

**Stay connected and informed – join our newsletter for the latest updates and insights - scan this QR code!**

**Need a consultation? Let's discuss your story - scan this QR code!**

# CONTENTS

Foreword 23

PART I: THE CRASHES THAT CHANGED MY LIFE

1 The Collisions that Changed it All 28

2 The Second Strike 32

3 The Long Road to Healing 36

4 Weathering the Legal Storm 39

5 Rising from the Rubble 41

6 The Echoes of the Impact 44

7 Infusing Empathy into Advocacy 47

PART II: A DETAILED GUIDE THROUGH THE AFTERMATH OF AN AUTO ACCIDENT

1 At the Scene of the Accident 53

2 Post-Accident Procedures 72

3 Legal Aspects of Auto Accidents 92

4 Managing Injuries and Medical Issues 106

5 The Financial Implications 129

6 Hiring a Personal Injury Attorney 142

7 Litigation and the Legal Process 152

8 My Closing Arguments 164

Share Your Story 165

# FOREWORD

My first brush with fate occurred after leaving a friend's wedding. I vividly remember the blaring green light as our SUV crossed the intersection, only to be violently struck. The sound of crushing metal and shattering glass echoed as the SUV spun uncontrollably, eventually landing on its side. Time slowed to a crawl; the chaos inside the vehicle was palpable. Blood splattered the ceilings and walls. My left shoulder, pinned against the door, bore the brunt of the impact. I remember gazing up at the sky, trapped and choking on the seatbelt. This day in 2006 marked the beginning of a life-altering journey for me as a personal injury attorney who built his career on advocating for those who suffered in accidents similar to the ones I would come to endure.

Beside me, my friend's wife was in a state of hysteria, fearing for her husband, who was in the front seat, his side of the car covered in blood. At that moment, our concussions seemed trivial against the backdrop of potential loss of life. The adrenaline that surged through my body numbed the pain, allowing me to crawl out and assist others. Surrounded by flashing lights and emergency personnel, the reality of our situation began to sink in.

The road to recovery was arduous. A nagging shoulder injury, initially masked by swelling, turned out to be a tear requiring surgery and extensive physical therapy. The exhausting battle of insurance claims created a nightmare that seemed endless. Unbeknownst to me, the experience was just a prelude to another incident that would further test my resilience.

Six years later, I was blindsided again. My life was seemingly back on track - married, expecting our first child, and setting up a new home. While waiting at a traffic light, a sudden impact catapulted my vehicle into a bustling intersection. In those seconds, I grappled with the frightening prospect of never meeting my unborn child, leaving my wife to raise our daughter alone. Miraculously, I survived the collision without a secondary impact. But the ordeal was far from over. Lying in the hospital boarded and neck braced, the discomfort was secondary to the emotional turmoil that engulfed me when my pregnant wife arrived. Every line of her face was etched in fear.

This second accident brought new challenges compared to the first one all those years ago. My claims were devalued by insurance companies citing "pre-existing" injuries. The subsequent legal battle was personal; deposed by colleagues, I had to lay bare my life's intimate details, endure skepticism about my suffering, and fight for justice against a system that seemed bent on breaking me down even further. I stood resolute in this battle, unwavering in my determination to confront and overcome the obstacles laid by the legal system.

These experiences shaped my approach as a personal injury attorney immeasurably. I understand, on a deeply personal level, the physical and emotional toll of accidents. The path to recovery is not simply physical; it's a journey of mental resilience, facing insurance companies and, sometimes, the legal system.

The empathy I extend to people is not just professional; it was born from shared experiences. I have lived the confusion, the pain, and the frustration. I know the importance of having someone who understands the legal intricacies, resonates with the personal struggle, and can relay that experience in the courtroom.

Beyond the legal arena, I am deeply intertwined with community engagement; from serving on local boards to supporting initiatives in West Baltimore, my passion is driven by the belief in the power of societal improvement and cohesion through community engagement. These experiences have shaped my worldview and reinforced the importance of family values and community support, two principles at the heart of my legal practice.

I crafted this guide from the lens of a lawyer who's not just versed in the technicalities of personal injury law but is also an active community member dedicated to making a positive impact. I designed the lessons and insights within these pages from my diverse experiences. I aim to provide you with a comprehensive understanding of navigating the complex aftermath of an auto accident.

As we journey through this book together, I hope that you gain the knowledge to manage the aftermath of an auto accident and the assurance that you are supported by a professional deeply invested in your recovery and well-being. Know that legal expertise and survivor's empathy guide you through the pages. I wrote these pages to be a beacon of hope for those who find their lives upended by the unforeseen and often unforgiving aftermath of a car accident. This text is not legal advice but life lessons from someone who has navigated the storm and emerged with a renewed purpose to advocate, empathize, and guide.

**This book is for informational purposes and is not legal advice**. If you have been involved in a motor vehicle collision, I strongly recommend contacting an experienced personal injury lawyer. Contact my firm at (410) 661-9440 or www.PinderPlotkin.com

# Part I

# The Crashes That Changed My Life

# 1. THE COLLISIONS THAT CHANGED IT ALL

Our SUV was violently struck - a cacophony of shattering glass and rending metal filled the air. In the harrowing moments after the first collision, the world seemed to tilt on its axis, throwing my body against the unforgiving hardness of the rear passenger door. Searing pain shot through my shoulder, only to be eclipsed by the choking grip of the seatbelt digging into my chest. I hung suspended, disoriented, and confused by the surreal sight of the sky where the window once was.

Flashback to the seconds before the chaos:

It was a night like any other, filled with the laughter and joy of a friend's wedding. The air was crisp, carrying the lingering scents of spring flowers and the sounds of distant celebration. Our spirits were high, oblivious to the life-altering event that lurked just a few blocks away. We drove through the quiet streets outside of Philadelphia, the green light at the intersection beckoning us forward as a silent harbinger of the chaos to come.

Without warning, a thunderous roar shattered our tranquility. Another vehicle, like a beast unleashed, careened into the side of our SUV. Time slowed to a crawl. The force of the impact hurled me against the door, a crushing weight against my left shoulder. The sound of crunching metal and breaking glass was deafening, a discordant symphony of destruction that resonated in my very bones and still does to this day.

The world spun wildly. Our SUV, once a haven of safety, was now a prisoner of physics, flipping onto its side. My senses were overwhelmed. The sharp, acrid smell of smoke and burnt rubber invaded my nostrils. I could hear the panicked screams of my friends, their voices distorted as if we were underwater. Fear was a tangible presence - a metallic tang on my tongue.

Trapped and disoriented, I gazed upwards, where the streetlights blurred into a hazy glow against the night sky. The seatbelt, my inadvertent savior, now constricted my chest, squeezing the breath from my lungs. I gasped for air with laborious breaths, each one a struggle. Chaos persisted all around me. Seated beside me, my friend's wife was a portrait of terror. Her eyes, wide with shock, were fixated on her husband's seat, where splatters of blood painted a gruesome picture against the canvas of the SUV's interior. Her hysterical sobs and the distant wail of sirens broke the eerie silence that followed the collision - shattering any semblance of safety.

Adrenaline surged, numbing my pain, and a primal instinct to survive took over. With trembling hands, I unclasped the seatbelt, an everyday action that felt monumental in my dazed state. Gravity reclaimed its hold, and I crumpled to the side of the SUV, now the roof. Glass crunched under me, even more evidence of the violent impact. Crawling through the shattered window, I emerged into a world that seemed alien, bathed in emergency vehicles' flashing red and blue lights. The cool night air was a harsh contrast to the stifling confines of the overturned SUV. With shaky hands, I reached back in and grasped my friend's wife, guiding her to the tenuous safety of the outside.

Sitting on the curb, we found a small island of refuge amidst the surrounding chaos. Emergency crews, moving with practiced urgency, stabilized the SUV to rescue the trapped passengers. The scene, surreal and etched with destruction and despair, would forever imprint itself in my memory.

In the days that followed, the true extent of my injuries became apparent. Beyond the initial shock and adrenaline, a deep, unrelenting pain took root in my shoulder. Doctors' visits and scans revealed a tear hidden beneath the swelling. A recovery plan was laid out before me - a daunting journey of surgery and physical therapy.

This accident - this violent upheaval of my life - was just the beginning of a season in my life that would test my resilience, challenge my perceptions, and, ultimately, redefine my purpose. The physical scars would heal in time, but the emotional wounds, the memories of that night, would leave an indelible mark on my soul.

As a personal injury attorney, I had always sympathized with my clients and understood their struggles in the aftermath of an accident as an outsider privy to intimate details. But after that night in 2006, I was no longer just a lawyer but a survivor. My experiences, though harrowing, granted me a deeper understanding and a more profound connection to those I would represent.

The collision marked a new chapter of my life, where my personal journey would become a beacon of hope for others navigating the tumultuous aftermath of their accidents. It was not just a story of survival. It was a testament to the human spirit's ability to endure and overcome. It was a reminder of the fragility of life, the unforeseen moments that can alter our paths irrevocably. In sharing my story, I hope to offer more than legal advice. I aim to provide solace, understanding, and a guiding hand through the darkness.

## 2. THE SECOND STRIKE

Six years had passed since that night - the night that accident redefined my existence. Those years were a mosaic of change, growth, and healing. I had embraced a new normal, where the echoes of the crash, the sound of the SUV crunching against the impact, lingered as mere whispers in the corners of my mind. With its remarkable resilience, life propelled me into love, marriage, and the joyous anticipation of fatherhood. Our world was expanding and bright with the promise of new beginnings.

It started as a day steeped in ordinary pursuits. I was on the hunt for a simple household item when fate struck again with its cruel penchant for unpredictability. The day was radiant, the sky above our little suburb in Baltimore a vast expanse of azure, unmarred by even a wisp of cloud. The air was alive with the hum of the city, the streets a symphony of the everyday. As I waited at a traffic light, my thoughts wandered to the future, the nursery that awaited completion, and the life we were eager to welcome. All I needed was a trash can - the first trash can for our new home.

In that moment of mundane reflection, calamity struck with a ferocity that shattered my world into a thousand unforgiving shards. It was as if a giant hand had swept my vehicle into the heart of a storm. The impact was sudden, an unyielding force that propelled my car into the chaos of the intersection. The sound of crunching metal was a grotesque echo of the past, a nightmare revisited with a vengeance. My body, once again, became a ragdoll in the hands of fate. The seatbelt, a deceptive guardian, restrained me even as it inflicted new agony. Pain erupted in my back and neck, a searing, white-hot intensity that threatened to engulf my consciousness. The world spun, a dizzying, terrifying carousel. Through the prism of my car's windows, I saw the approaching vehicles, their faces distorted, their part in this event unintentionally lethal.

Once more, time slowed to a torturous crawl. In those elongated seconds, my life flashed before my eyes - not in the cliched montage of memories, but in the acute realization of all that could be lost. Images of my wife, radiant with the life we had created, juxtaposed with the crushing fear of never holding my child, of leaving my partner to navigate the world alone. The weight of these unspoken goodbyes pressed upon me, heavier than the wrecked steel encasing me.

By some inexplicable grace, the anticipated impact of oncoming traffic never came. The clamor around me gradually dimmed, replaced by a ringing silence that pulsed in my ears. I was alive, yet the relief was transient, quickly overshadowed by the onslaught of pain and the encroaching tide of realization.

The extraction from my vehicle was a blur of faces and voices, a whirlwind of motion that seemed simultaneously frantic and painfully slow. The paramedic's faces, etched with concern and professionalism, maneuvered me onto a board with clinical efficiency. The hardness of the board and the constricting embrace of the neck brace were each stark reminders of my vulnerability and the unpredictability of the world. Lying there, immobilized, the hospital's sterile ceiling offered no comfort as my mind raced, trapped in a whirlwind of worry for my unborn child, for the wife who had become my world. When she appeared, her face a canvas of fear and love, the dam holding back my emotions broke. Tears, unbidden and unstoppable, streamed down my face - each one a testament to the fragility of our carefully constructed happiness.

The journey that followed was an odyssey of recovery and frustration. The physical injuries, though less catastrophic than they might have been, were compounded by the psychological scars. Sleep became elusive, chased away by the aches, pains, and uncertainties that lurked in the shadows. The legal battle that ensued was a different beast altogether. Confronted with the complexities of insurance claims and the harsh realities of pre-existing conditions, I found myself on the other side of the courtroom - not as an attorney, but as a victim, my integrity and pain under scrutiny.

The grueling hours of depositions and the probing questions of colleagues, now adversaries, were invading the most private corners of my life. To have one's suffering dissected, quantified, and judged was a humiliation that transcended physical pain. It was a battle not just for compensation but for validation, for acknowledgment of the unseen wounds that the accident had inflicted upon my family and me.

Through this crucible - this agonizing predicament - of pain and litigation, my perspective as a lawyer was irrevocably altered. The empathy I had always prided myself on deepened into a visceral understanding. I lived the nightmare that my clients faced and navigated the labyrinth of recovery and justice, just like they are seeking. This shared experience became the cornerstone of my practice, the guiding principle that informed every case, every client interaction, and every decision in the courtroom.

The aftermath of these collisions shaped my life in ways I could never have anticipated. The physical scars healed, leaving faint traces that went skin-deep, yet the emotional and psychological impact of these events lingered, weaving themselves into the very fabric of my being. These experiences did not just change me; they redefined the essence of my empathy and advocacy. As a lawyer and as a human being, I emerged from these trials with a renewed commitment to champion the cause of those who, like me, had their lives turned upside down in an instant. This journey, fraught with pain and enlightenment, forged a path where my personal ordeal became a beacon of hope and understanding for others facing similar battles.

# 3. THE LONG ROAD TO HEALING

In the wake of the second collision, my world became a vortex of chaos and pain all over again. The aftermath was a maze of physical therapy sessions, each one a grueling testament to the injuries inflicted upon my body. The therapists' hands, skilled yet impersonal, prodded the tender areas of my back and neck, seeking to undo the damage wrought by unyielding steel and gravity. Each stretch and exercise were a battle, a painful reminder of my fragility.

The therapy room became my sanctuary but also my prison. The scent of antiseptic mingled with the faint odor of sweat and determination lingered around me while other patients fought their battles, their faces etched with a mixture of pain and resolve. We were a silent fraternity, bound by the common pursuit of reclaiming our lives from the clutches of injury.

Aqua therapy sessions offered a temporary respite, the buoyancy of the water a gentle reprieve from the relentless pull of gravity. Yet even there, amidst the soothing embrace of warm water, the shadows of the accident followed me. Each movement was a reflection in the pool's mirror-like surface, a distorted echo of the person I had once been.

The road to recovery extended far beyond the physical realm; it was also a profound mental and emotional journey. The impact of the accidents resonated deep within my subconscious, affecting every facet of my existence. Nights were particularly agonizing. I would lay awake, tormented by relentless pain that seemed to echo the severity of the collisions. Sleep, once a restful escape, became an elusive luxury, frequently disrupted by the persistent, throbbing reminder of my injuries. The sounds of the accidents — the harsh screeching of tires and the violent shattering of glass — seemed to replay in my mind, but it was the unyielding physical discomfort that genuinely kept me from peace.

My family, my unwavering support system, helplessly watched as I grappled with the invisible demons. My compassionate wife was a beacon of hope and strength amidst the storm. But even then, I saw the worry in her eyes, the unspoken fears for our future and our growing family's wellbeing. Our conversations, once filled with plans and laughter, our conversations were now tinged with the unspoken acknowledgment of our altered reality.

---

As an attorney, I prided myself on my resilience and ability to advocate for those wronged. But these experiences humbled me; they stripped me down to my core. I understood, in a way I never had before, the true impact of a personal injury. It was not just about the broken bones or the medical bills; it was about the stolen moments, the dreams deferred, the uncertainty that clouded every aspect of life.

Through this journey, I gained a profound empathy for my clients. I saw in their eyes the same fears and struggles I still faced. My pain became a bridge, connecting us in a way beyond legal representation. It was a connection forged in the fires of shared experience, a bond that lent depth and sincerity to my advocacy. I found a newfound purpose as I navigated the complex dance of recovery and litigation. I became more than just a lawyer; I was a guide, a fellow traveler on a road that I knew all too well. In sharing my story, I hoped to offer not just legal counsel but a measure of comfort as well - reassurance that they were not alone in their journey.

This chapter of my life was more than a tale of accidents and injuries; it was a story of resilience, of rediscovering strength in the face of adversity. It was a testament to the enduring spirit of the human heart, a heart that beats with the relentless rhythm of hope after a life-altering car accident.

# 4. WEATHERING THE LEGAL STORM

The aftermath of the collisions plunged me into a legal whirlwind, a world in which my physical injuries were joined with the emotional turmoil of fighting for justice. The legal battles were not just a fight for compensation; they were a struggle for recognition of the profound impact these accidents had on my life and the lives of those I loved.

The familiar setting took on an entirely different perspective when I entered the discovery phase. The air was thick with tension, a tangible reminder of the high stakes laid before me. The depositions were a particularly harrowing ordeal. Seated in a stark room under the unblinking gaze of the opposing counsel, I felt exposed and vulnerable. Each question was a probe into my most intimate experiences of pain and loss. Though truthful and heartfelt, my answers seemed to evaporate in the clinical atmosphere of the room. The opposing lawyers, once colleagues, now bore the masks of adversaries, their questions sharp and unrelenting.

The inquiries and nitpicking into my physical and emotional state felt like a re-opening of wounds that had barely begun to heal. The descriptions of the accidents were recounted in excruciating detail, each word a reminder of the terror and pain that enveloped me on those fateful days. The memories, still vivid and raw, played out in my mind's eye, a relentless replay of metal colliding, glass shattering, and the world spinning out of control. As I sat there, recounting the events, I could feel a palpable undercurrent of skepticism, a barrier erected by the stigma attached to personal injury claims and the profession I represented. It was a painful irony that I, who had dedicated my life to advocating for others, now had to fight to legitimize my own suffering.

The journey through the legal system was arduous and draining, both physically and mentally. Once familiar and welcoming, the corridors of litigation now felt like a malicious labyrinth, each turn leading me deeper into a maze of legal complexities and emotional upheaval. Yet, through this ordeal, I gleaned invaluable insights into the plight of my clients. I experienced firsthand the frustration of being entangled in legal proceedings, the feeling of being a mere case number rather than a human being grappling with trauma. This experience deepened my resolve to be more than just a lawyer but an advocate and voice for those silenced by injury and loss.

The relief was palpable as the legal battles drew to a close, with settlements reached. However, it was not the triumph of a victory that stayed with me, but the profound realization of the resilience of the human spirit. The experience had transformed me, not just as an attorney but as a person. I emerged from the legal storm with renewed purpose and a tangible empathy for those I represented. The scars of the accidents, both visible and invisible, became a part of me, a testament to survival and a reminder that life is fragile but also carries a silent strength.

# 5. RISING FROM THE RUBBLE

Emerging from the legal tumult, I found myself standing at the crossroads of recovery and reinvention. The collisions hadn't just left physical scars; they had fundamentally altered the trajectory of my life. Each day became a testament to resilience, a new chapter of rediscovering my strength amidst vulnerability.

The healing process was akin to navigating through a dense fog. I would have moments of clarity interspersed with periods of overwhelming uncertainty. My body, once a vessel of strength and reliability, had become a patchwork of healed fractures and rehabilitated muscles. The mirror reflected a version of myself that bore the subtle yet indelible marks of survival - the faint lines, the slightly altered posture, the cautious movements.

Yet, it was in the quiet solitude of reflection where the deeper transformation occurred. The injuries, while healing, had sown seeds of introspection, germinating into a profound understanding of the fragility of life. The moments spent in the cocoon of recovery were not just about mending broken bones; they were about weaving the tapestry of a new identity.

My perspective as a personal injury attorney underwent a metamorphosis in this reinvention. The courtroom was once a battleground of legal prowess but now resonated with a deeper purpose. Each case I undertook became a narrative, not just of legal arguments and evidence, but of human resilience and the quest for justice. My clients' stories were no longer abstract scenarios; they were reflections of my journey, echoes of the shared experience of pain, struggle, and survival.

This newfound empathy transformed the way I connected with my clients. As a kindred spirit, I listened to their stories with an understanding of the unspoken fears and the silent cries of frustration. Each meeting was not just a legal consultation but an exchange of shared humanity, a mutual recognition of the odyssey from victim to survivor. The experience of being a victim stripped away my expertly crafted veneer of professional detachment. The pain, the fear, and the uncertainty I had endured resonated in the narratives of those I represented. It was as if each case was a piece of my own story, a chapter in the grander book of collective struggle against unforeseen adversity.

My role as an attorney took on a new dimension in the aftermath of the collisions. I became a guardian of stories, a steward of the journey from injury to recovery. I approached each case imbued with a more profound sense of purpose and an unwavering commitment to not just legal success but to the holistic well-being of my clients outside of the courtroom.

Navigating through this newly transformed landscape, I continued to feel the echoes of the accidents resonating within me. These were not merely memories of trauma; they became the crucible that reforged my purpose. The empathy, understanding, and commitment I now bring to my practice are not just professional attributes; they are the hard-earned fruits of my personal trials.

The journey from the rubble of the accidents to the resurgence of a new self was a path lined with challenges and revelations. It was a testament to the enduring human capacity to rise from adversity to rebuild amidst ruins. In sharing my story, I hoped to offer more than legal advice; I aspired to provide a beacon of hope, a reminder that even in the depths of despair, there is a potential for rebirth, a chance to emerge stronger, wiser, and more compassionate.

# 6. THE ECHOES OF THE IMPACT

As the chapters of my life unfolded after the collisions, the echoes of those defining moments lingered, reverberating through each day in memories like dark shadows trailing me. Each one was a reminder of life's fragility and how suddenly something can alter it.

The physical aftermath of the accidents brought lingering pain and continuously cautious movements. Each step, each turn of my body, was a conscious effort dictated by the memory of injuries that once debilitated me. The once simple acts of bending to embrace my child or reaching for a loved one became measured exercises, tinged with an awareness of vulnerability and the fear of re-injury.

I often found myself lost in reflection in the quiet moments of solitude. My mind would wander back to those split seconds that changed everything—the blinding flash of impact, the disorienting spin of the vehicle, and the oppressive tightness of the seatbelt that both restrained and saved me. These recollections were not just mental images; they were visceral experiences, reignited with every recall and sent shivers down my spine.

The emotional scars ran even deeper. There was an undercurrent of anxiety that accompanied me, an unwelcome companion on my journey. The simple act of driving, once a mundane part of daily life, was now a venture fraught with tension whenever I drove past the fateful intersection.

This lingering anxiety was a silent struggle; I felt its oppressive weight in moments of supposed safety. In conversations with friends or amid a busy workday, the specter of the accidents would sometimes surface, a sudden jolt of fear triggered by a sound or a movement, a flashback to those moments of chaos and helplessness.

And yet, even amidst the challenges, the fruits of resilience began to bloom.

My family became a pillar of strength and dependability. The experience of the accidents brought us closer, forging bonds of understanding and mutual support. We celebrated the small victories together—the successful completion of a therapy session, the return to a beloved activity, and the simple joy of a pain-free day. The journey through the aftermath of a car accident is not just a physical recovery; it's a process of rebuilding, of finding a new normal amidst the changed landscape of one's life.

The lessons learned from the crashes extended beyond the physical and legal realms. They taught me about the resilience of the human spirit, the capacity to endure and adapt, and the power of empathy. These experiences shaped me as a lawyer and a person, imbuing me with a profound appreciation for each moment and a deep-seated desire to help others navigate their paths through adversity.

Reflecting on those moments of impact, I see them as points of collision and as catalysts for transformation. This transformation allowed me to emerge not broken but reshaped, fortified by the trials, and ready to face the challenges and opportunities that lie ahead.  I survived and returned to my daily life, and so can you!

# 7. INFUSING EMPATHY INTO ADVOCACY

In the wake of my harrowing experiences, the essence of my personal and professional identity underwent a profound metamorphosis. The violent collisions, marked by the shattering of glass and the brutal distortion of metal, did more than inflict physical wounds; they reshaped my perspective on life and fundamentally altered my approach to practicing law.

I paved the road to this understanding through relentless physical pain, emotional turbulence, and the daunting task of navigating the legal system from a client's perspective. What was once familiar and predictable seemed like someone had infused my world with a deeper significance. Simple joys turned into profound treasures, and the bonds of family and friendship became my lifelines in navigating through my darkest moments.

Emerging from this chapter of chaos and recovery, I embraced a renewed mission - to mentor my legal team in the art of empathetic advocacy, ensuring that we fight fiercely for our clients' compensation and become the voice of their ordeal. As a mentor to the legal team, I emphasized the importance of seeing our clients as more than just case numbers or legal challenges. I reminded them that these clients are individuals who have suffered through traumatic experiences and had their lives changed by unforeseen disasters. I urged my team to genuinely listen to our client's stories of injury and loss and grasp the emotional and psychological impact.

Our firm cultivated an atmosphere where empathy was as crucial as legal expertise. I shared vivid memories of my accidents in team meetings, describing the sensory overload of each collision - the deafening roar of impact, the disorienting sensation of the world spinning out of control, and the oppressive weight of fear and uncertainty that followed. These stories served as powerful reminders to my team that behind every case file lay a human story marked by similar fears, pain, and upheaval.

I taught them how to be effective advocates. We needed to connect with our clients on a human level. It was essential to understand the facts of the case *and* the personal narratives that accompanied them. This understanding allowed us to represent our clients with legal acumen and a passion and commitment born from a place of genuine understanding and shared experience.

Moreover, I stressed the importance of being our clients' voice. Many clients came to us feeling voiceless and overwhelmed; the overwhelming legal proceedings and insurance negotiations drowned out their stories. Our role was to amplify their voices, to ensure that somebody heard their story and acknowledged their suffering. This approach went beyond seeking compensation; it was about seeking justice and validation for the ordeals they had endured.

I regularly conducted workshops for my team, focusing on the nuances of empathetic communication and client relations. We delved into case studies, analyzing the legal strategies and the emotional dynamics at play in the situations. These sessions were instrumental in developing a team of attorneys who were skilled in the courtroom and relayed compassion and understanding during client interactions.

In my mentorship, I emphasized the power of storytelling in the courtroom. I taught my team how to weave the facts of the case into compelling narratives that resonated with juries and judges alike. These narratives were more than legal arguments; they were accounts of resilience and the fight for justice, and they often made the difference in achieving favorable outcomes for our clients.

I led by example, taking on challenging cases and demonstrating how a blend of empathy and legal prowess could yield remarkable results. My door was always open, not just for legal discussions but also for conversations about the emotional aspects of our work. I shared my struggles and successes, creating a space where vulnerability was not a weakness but a strength - something uncommon in our line of work. Due to this change, the team learned to view each case through a lens of compassion, understanding that our clients entrusted us with not just their legal battles but also their hopes and fears. We became more than lawyers; we were allies.

In every case we handled, we strived to honor the trust placed in us. We fought tirelessly to maximize compensation, but more importantly, we fought to ensure that our clients felt seen, heard, and respected. We tailored our legal strategies to reflect the financial losses and the full spectrum of our clients' experiences - the physical pain, the emotional anguish, and the impact on their daily lives.

This profound shift in our practice wasn't just about refining legal strategies but also redefining the essence of legal advocacy. Our commitment went beyond the courtroom; it extended into the very lives of those we represented. We stood as fierce defenders of their rights but equally as compassionate listeners to their stories, validating their experiences and acknowledging their pain.

Our firm's culture became one in which fierce advocacy and deep empathy coexisted harmoniously; it was about acknowledging their pain, supporting their journey to recovery, and restoring a sense of dignity and hope many had lost in the aftermath of their accidents. In every interaction, in every case, we strived to maximize compensation and restore our clients a sense of justice and dignity. We measured our success in settlements or verdicts, the trust we built, and the lives we touched. This transformation, born from the depths of my own experiences, created a legacy of empathy and fierce advocacy, marking our firm as a beacon of hope and a stronghold of understanding in the legal community.

In the tapestry of my experiences, woven through with resilience, pain, and triumph, I have found a defining truth that has become our firm's guiding motto: Hardworking Attorneys for Hardworking People®. This statement is a testament to the enduring spirit and relentless determination that guide us through life's most formidable challenges.

---

Now that you've journeyed through my story, I'm eager to hear yours. Share your experiences with me and let's continue this conversation together.

# Part 2

# A Detailed Guide Through the Aftermath of an Auto Accident

# 1. AT THE SCENE OF THE ACCIDENT

An auto accident, even a minor one, can be a disorienting and stressful experience. The moments immediately following the crash are critical for your physical safety and the legal and financial implications that may follow. This chapter provides a step-by-step guide on what to do immediately after an accident, helping you navigate this challenging situation with clarity and confidence.

## Immediate Steps After an Accident

When you're involved in an auto accident, your immediate priority should always be safety. The actions you take depend significantly on the nature of the accident and its location. If you're involved in a minor collision where your vehicle is still operational and poses a risk of obstructing traffic, carefully move it to the roadside or another safe area. Doing this helps prevent any additional accidents and clears the way for emergency vehicles if they need to pass.

**PRO TIP:**

Move everything out of the way *after* taking pictures and videos documenting the position of the vehicles and the roadway.

Scenarios in which moving your vehicle isn't possible, however — either due to severe damage, personal injury, or both — turn on your hazard lights. Doing this is especially crucial to warn other drivers of your presence in poor visibility conditions, at night, or in bad weather.

### Specific Considerations to be Aware Of

**Busy Intersections**: In accidents occurring at intersections, swift action is critical to avoid further incidents. If somebody can move the vehicles, do so promptly. If not, set up warning signals and wait for law enforcement inside your car.

**Highways**: High-speed roads pose a greater risk post-accident. If you cannot move your vehicle off the highway, stay inside with seat belts fastened and hazards on, as exiting the car could be more dangerous due to fast-moving traffic.

**Rural Areas**: In less populated areas, where traffic is lighter, and help might take longer, ensure your vehicle is visible to passing drivers. Use any available safety markers or flares if you have them. Having a well-stocked emergency kit in your car can be invaluable in these situations.

In any scenario, once safety measures are in place, check yourself and your passengers for injuries. Even if the accident seems minor, injuries can be hidden or delayed in their onset. Assessing and ensuring everyone's safety is the first critical step in handling the aftermath of an auto accident.

### Assessing Injuries

In the wake of an auto accident, the initial moments are crucial for assessing injuries to yourself and any passengers involved. It's essential to understand that the shock and adrenaline surge experienced during such traumatic events can often mask pain, leading to a delayed onset of injury symptoms. Consequently, injuries might not be immediately noticeable or might seem less severe than they are. This phenomenon can dangerously downplay the need for immediate medical attention. I have first-hand experience with the shock and adrenaline that goes through your body after a collision - that, plus concussion symptoms, can impact your decision-making and mask the physical and psychological impact of the crash.

Your first step is a quick but thorough self-assessment and check on all passengers. Pay attention to any pain, discomfort, or disorientation, no matter how mild they appear initially. Remember, in the context of an auto accident, there is no such thing as being overly cautious. Even seemingly minor injuries should prompt a call to 911. The urgency of getting a medical evaluation cannot be overstated, as some severe injuries, such as internal bleeding or concussions, may not be immediately apparent.

**Let's dive into different types of injuries commonly sustained in auto accidents and their signs:**

**Whiplash**: Often occurring in rear-end collisions, whiplash is a neck injury due to forceful, rapid back-and-forth movement of the neck, like the cracking of a whip. Symptoms can include neck pain and stiffness, headaches at the base of the skull, dizziness, and sometimes blurred vision.

**Concussions**: A concussion is a traumatic brain injury that affects brain function. Signs can include headaches, memory problems, confusion, drowsiness or feeling sluggish, dizziness, double or blurry vision, nausea, and sensitivity to light or noise.

**Broken Bones and Fractures**: The sudden impact of a car accident can cause various fractures and broken bones. Symptoms include intense pain at the injury site, swelling or bruising, deformity, inability to move the affected limb, and, in some cases, the bone protruding through the skin.

**Internal Bleeding**: This is a less apparent but potentially life-threatening injury. Symptoms might include abdominal pain and swelling, dizziness or fainting, large areas of deep purple bruising, numbness in extremities, and low blood pressure.

**Soft Tissue Injuries**: These are injuries to muscles, ligaments, and tendons and can include sprains, strains, or tears. Symptoms may include pain, swelling, bruising, and loss of function at the injury site.

**Cuts and Lacerations**: Broken glass or metal can cause cuts, which may be superficial or deep. Signs include bleeding, pain, and visible opening of the skin. It's important to control bleeding and prevent infection. Wrap any severe wound to staunch the bleeding.

**Spinal Cord Injuries**: These injuries can range from minor ligament and muscle strains to fractures and dislocations of the vertebrae. Symptoms can include severe pain, pressure, stiffness, muscle weakness, and, in severe cases, loss of movement or sensation below the injury site.

**Psychological Trauma**: It's also important to acknowledge the potential for psychological trauma following a car accident. Symptoms might include persistent anxiety, stress, fear of driving, sleep disturbances, or mood swings.

In all these cases, immediate medical attention is paramount. Even if you or your passengers feel fine, some injuries have delayed symptoms and can lead to complications if left untreated. It's always better to err on caution and undergo a professional medical evaluation following an accident. This approach ensures that any injuries, apparent or not, are appropriately addressed, thus safeguarding your health and well-being in the aftermath of an auto accident.

### Get Ahold of Emergency Services

In the immediate aftermath of an auto accident, one of your first actions should be to dial 911. This step is crucial, regardless of the accident's apparent severity. Once connected with the emergency operator, providing detailed and precise information is essential. This information includes your exact location – use road names, mile markers, or any notable landmarks to help emergency services locate you quickly. Mention the number of vehicles involved in the accident. Be clear about any visible injuries to yourself, passengers, or others involved in the accident. Even if the injuries seem minor, it's essential to report them.

When the accident appears minor, and no one is hurt, you might wonder whether calling 911 is necessary. The answer is yes; it is always advisable. A key reason for this is the importance of obtaining a police report. Even in less severe accidents, a police report serves as an official and objective record of the incident.

**There are a few reasons why a police report is utterly indispensable:**

**Official Documentation**: A police report provides an unbiased record of the accident's events. Insurance companies rely on an authoritative document to determine fault and liability.

**Insurance Claims**: When filing an insurance claim, a police report can expedite the process. It offers your insurance company a detailed account of the accident, which can be crucial, especially in cases where the other party disputes your version of the events.

**Legal Protection**: Should legal issues arise from the accident, a police report is a valuable asset. It offers a factual basis for any court proceedings, providing an account from a law enforcement officer's perspective.

**Fault and Liability Clarification**: The report may include the responding officer's assessment of the accident, often noting any violated traffic laws. This document can be instrumental in determining fault and liability.

**Witness Statements**: Police reports often contain statements from witnesses. These objective accounts can be pivotal in insurance and legal proceedings.

**Accurate Details**: In the chaos that often follows an accident, details can become confused. A police report accurately captures the information, including date, time, weather, and road conditions.

**Injury Documentation**: Even if injuries are not apparent immediately, the report can document any claims of pain or discomfort, which can be essential if medical issues arise later.

**Damage Assessment**: The report records the vehicle damage involved, which can be crucial for insurance claims.

**Ensure the police report contains the following:**

- The date, time, and location of the accident.
- All parties' personal details: names, addresses, phone numbers, insurance information.
- Descriptions of the vehicles involved: make, model, color, and license plate numbers.
- Statements from drivers, passengers, and witnesses.
- The officer's observation of damages and injuries.
- An initial assessment of fault and any citations issued.
- Diagrams or sketches of the accident scene.

To sum it up, a police report is vital in the aftermath of an auto accident. It provides a reliable and objective record that can be critical in dealing with insurance claims and any legal proceedings that may follow. Remember, ensuring that the police file is thorough and accurate can significantly impact the resolution of your accident in terms of both insurance and legal matters. Gathering all the details, you can be worth it in the end!

## Interacting with Other Parties Involved

If the police cannot come to the scene, exchanging essential information with the other driver involved is crucial. This step is critical, regardless of who might be at fault. The information exchanged should include each driver's full name, contact number, address, insurance company name, policy number, and details about their vehicle, such as the make, model, color, and license plate number. It's equally crucial to understand the nuances of how the parties should exchange information and the nature of communication with the other driver and any bystanders present.

Approach the situation with a level of calm and composure. Understandably, emotions can run high after an accident, but remaining calm is essential. When speaking with the other driver, be courteous and respectful. Avoid engaging in aggressive behavior, even if the other party is agitated.

Remember to avoid discussing the details of the accident itself. Doing this means not admitting fault or making statements that could imply guilt, such as "I didn't see you" or "I'm sorry." These kinds of remarks, however well-intentioned, can be interpreted as admissions of liability and could significantly impact the insurance claims process or any legal proceedings that may follow. Stick strictly to the exchange of factual information.

When talking to bystanders, remember that their accounts might later be as crucial as witness statements. Thus, similar rules apply: avoid discussing details or admitting fault and keep interactions straightforward and fact-based.

Knowing what not to say during these interactions is equally crucial. Avoid making speculative statements about the cause of the accident or discussing specifics about your insurance policy, like coverage limits. It's not the time to negotiate or resolve who's at fault; insurance companies and possibly legal counsel will settle that matter later.

Be mindful of your body language as well. Non-verbal cues can often communicate more than words in a tense situation. Maintain a neutral posture and tone of voice to avoid miscommunication.

If the other driver is uncooperative or refuses to provide their information, remain calm. It's important not to escalate the situation. Simply note down their vehicle's license plate and any other observable details. This information, along with the police report and any witness statements, will be valuable in the insurance claims process.

Remember to also gather as much evidence as you can at the scene. This includes taking photos of both vehicles and the accident site, which can clearly record the conditions and damages involved. Ultimately, the exchange of information after an auto accident should be handled with care, focusing on collecting necessary details while avoiding discussions or admissions that could impact future claims or legal actions. Keeping communication clear, factual, and non-confrontational is key to protecting your interests in the aftermath of an accident.

## Documenting the Scene

In the aftermath of an auto accident, proper documentation is not just helpful; it's essential. Comprehensive photography is one of the most effective ways to document the scene. Capturing the right images can significantly aid in the insurance claim process and legal proceedings and ensure a fair and accurate account of events.

### What to Photograph

**All Vehicles Involved**: Take clear pictures of all vehicles involved in the accident from various angles, not just the areas directly impacted. This helps to counter any claims that pre-existing damages resulted from the accident. Capture the overall context of the accident and close-ups of the damage to each vehicle.

**Road and Weather Conditions**: Photograph the road layout, any skid marks, and the condition of the road. This could include puddles, ice, or debris that might have contributed to the accident. Weather conditions can also be critical, so capture elements that indicate weather conditions at the time of the accident.

**Street Signs and Traffic Signals**: Capture nearby street signs, traffic lights, or other road markers. These resources help establish the exact location of the accident and clarify right-of-way or other traffic rules that may be relevant.

**PRO TIP**:

Take pictures of the cars that stop at the accident scene. Make sure their license plates are visible. Your attorney can do a vehicle tag search to identify the witnesses if they are needed.

### Effective Photography Techniques

**Multiple Angles**: Take photos from various angles and distances to comprehensively view the accident. This includes wide shots to capture the entire scene and closer shots for specific details.

**Use of Perspective**: Try to include some everyday objects for scale to give a sense of size and distance. For instance, a traffic cone or a street sign beside a skid mark can provide a scale reference.

**Lighting**: Ensure there is adequate lighting. If the accident happens at night, use your vehicle's headlights, streetlights, or flashlights to illuminate dark areas.

**Avoiding Glare**: Be mindful of glare, especially when photographing vehicle damage. Different angles can help mitigate glare from the sun or reflective surfaces.

**Sequential Approach**: Start with wide shots of the entire scene and then progressively move closer to document specific details like vehicle damage, road conditions, and injuries.

**Photographing Injuries**: If there are visible injuries, photograph them as well. However, always prioritize medical attention over documenting injuries.

**Unaltered Scenes**: Take photos before any vehicles or debris are moved. This gives an accurate representation of the accident at the moment of impact.

**Use your Technology**: Most smartphones have high-quality cameras. Different features such as flash, HDR, or panoramic views are used to capture better-quality pictures.

**Backup and Storage**: Ensure that you back up these photos as soon as possible. Using cloud storage or emailing the pictures to yourself can prevent the loss of these crucial pieces of evidence.

All in all, the photographs you take at the scene of an auto accident can be pivotal in supporting your account of the incident. They provide tangible evidence that clarifies details, establishes facts, and influences the outcome of insurance claims and legal disputes. Remember, these images supplement your version of the events, adding credibility and precision to your accident narrative. Keep a backup copy in cloud storage even if you provide your attorney with the photographs. Image files can become corrupted, and the backup could make a world of difference in your case.

## Gathering Witness Information

Witnesses can play a constructive role in the aftermath of an auto accident. Their first-hand accounts often prove invaluable during insurance claims and legal proceedings. When approaching potential witnesses, it's essential to do so with courtesy and respect for their willingness to help.

Start by politely introducing yourself and briefly explaining your involvement in the accident. Ask if they would be comfortable providing their contact information — including their name, phone number, and address. This ensures that you or your legal representative can contact them later for a more detailed account.

If a witness is ready to share their observations, encourage them to provide a brief but precise description. However, be mindful not to pressure or lead them in their recounting. The goal is to gather honest and unfiltered observations.

When documenting witness statements, focus on capturing the specifics of what they saw before, during, and after the collision. Key details can include the direction of the vehicles, speed, traffic signals, and any actions or reactions of the drivers involved. Remember, witness accounts can significantly impact interpreting the accident's events, offering a perspective that might differ from those directly involved. Their statements can help construct a more complete and accurate picture of the incident.

**PRO TIP**:

In a recent incident, a client involved in a distressing collision wisely made three crucial calls: first to 911, then to a family member, and finally to me, directly from the accident scene. Despite being in pain from the deployed airbags – which thankfully saved her – she managed to stay composed enough to follow my guidance. As a witness came forward, I advised having them capture photos of the scene. This quick action ensured the preservation of vital evidence, especially as my client had to be swiftly transported to the hospital by paramedics and couldn't safely exit her vehicle to document the scene herself.

### Cooperating with Law Enforcement

Effective communication and interaction with law enforcement is critical to handling an auto accident. When officers arrive at the scene, they are there to assess the situation, gather information, and create an official report. Your cooperation and honesty are vital to this process.

Start by calmly providing a clear and factual account of the events as you recall them. Stick to the facts, avoiding any speculation or assumptions about what might have caused the accident or who might be at fault. It's essential to be straightforward in your responses, but if there are details you're uncertain about, it's perfectly acceptable to acknowledge that. Guessing or providing inaccurate information can complicate matters.

Remember, the responding officer's report is not just a formality. It plays a substantial role in the incident's aftermath, particularly in insurance claims and potential legal proceedings. This report will be used to determine the facts and circumstances surrounding the accident and can significantly influence the resolution of any disputes.

Clarity and honesty should be your guiding principles when speaking with law enforcement. Clear communication can help ensure that the report is as accurate and detailed as possible, providing a solid foundation for any necessary follow-up actions.

**PRO TIP**:

There are times when victims of car accidents are quickly taken to the hospital, missing the chance to talk with the law enforcement officer on the scene. Should the accident report turn out to be vague or not in their favor, it's advisable for the victim to reach out to the officer to request an addendum, ensuring their side of the story is included. However, it's crucial to first seek advice from an attorney before making this contact. This approach ensures that any additional statements are made under proper legal guidance.

### Medical Attention

In the moments following an auto accident, the adrenaline rush and immediate shock can often mask pain and injury. It is a common misconception that if one feels fine right after an accident, medical attention is not needed. However, seeking medical care in the aftermath of an auto accident is crucial for everyone, not only for addressing immediate injuries but also as a necessary precaution to hidden or delayed injuries. This section expands on the importance of medical attention, documentation, and follow-ups post-accident.

### Immediate Medical Evaluation

The initial step after an accident should be to undergo a medical evaluation, even if there are no obvious signs of injury. Some common injuries from auto accidents, such as whiplash, concussions, or internal injuries, may not present immediate symptoms. In fact, it's not uncommon for injury symptoms to manifest days or even weeks later. Immediate medical attention ensures that any hidden injuries are diagnosed and treated promptly, reducing the risk of complications.

### Documenting Your Injuries

Medical documentation is essential in any subsequent insurance claim or legal case. This documentation creates an official record of your injuries and treatment, which is crucial for several reasons.

**Proof of Injury**: Medical records prove that your injuries directly resulted from the accident. This is particularly important in cases where the extent or cause of injuries might be disputed.

**Detailing the Extent of Injuries**: Detailed medical records provide a clear picture of the severity of your injuries. This information can be critical in quantifying the damages in an insurance claim or lawsuit. DO NOT be a superhero. Make sure you reference all injuries, no matter how small. Think back to my story; that nagging shoulder injury was barely mentioned for the first six months - the KEY for causation was that it was mentioned!

**Treatment and Recovery Timeline**: Medical records outline your treatment plan and recovery process. This information can help claim compensation for medical expenses and be significant in cases where long-term care or rehabilitation is needed.

**Causality and Liability**: In some cases, the opposing insurance company or parties involved might challenge the causality of the injuries. Comprehensive medical documentation helps establish a clear link between the accident and your injuries.

## The Importance of Follow-Up Appointments

Follow-up appointments are just as necessary as the initial medical examination. They serve several purposes:

**Monitor Your Recovery**: Regular follow-ups help monitor your recovery and ensure the injuries heal as expected. They also provide an opportunity to adjust treatment plans if needed.

**Document Ongoing Issues**: Continuous medical records are essential in demonstrating the lasting effects of your injuries. This persistent documentation is vital in cases where injuries lead to long-term or permanent damage.

**Evidence of Compliance**: Attending all scheduled appointments and adhering to prescribed treatments demonstrates your commitment to recovery. This can be important in legal cases, as it shows that you have taken all necessary steps to mitigate the impact of your injuries.

## Managing Long-Term Health Concerns

In cases of severe accidents, injuries might lead to long-term health issues, which can significantly impact your life. Chronic pain, mobility issues, or cognitive impairments are some examples. Regular medical check-ups and consultations with specialists are important in managing these long-term effects. They also contribute to a continuous medical record that reflects the ongoing impact of the accident on your life.

**PRO TIP**:

In certain states, including Maryland, there's a legal obligation for accident victims to mitigate their damages. This essentially means that insurance companies may contend that your injuries would have healed more rapidly or wouldn't have become chronic had you consistently sought medical treatment. As an experienced professional, I can attest to witnessing insurance adjusters and attorneys assert these bold claims without batting an eye. It's part of their role, and they perform it with immense skill. Remember, regular medical follow-ups are not just crucial for your health but also a strategic move in your legal journey.

### Dealing with Psychological Impact

Acknowledging the psychological impact of being involved in an auto accident is crucial. Conditions such as post-traumatic stress disorder (PTSD), anxiety, and depression are common among accident victims. Seeking help from mental health professionals is as important as treating physical injuries. Documenting any psychological treatment and its relation to the accident can be important, particularly in cases where emotional distress damages are claimed.

### Navigating Insurance and Legal Processes

Detailed and thorough medical documentation is your most vital asset in dealing with insurance claims or legal cases post-accident. It provides a clear, undeniable record of the injuries sustained and the treatments required as a result of the accident. In many cases, the amount of compensation you receive is directly related to the extent and severity of injuries as documented in your medical records.

I cannot overstress how to pursue prompt and thorough medical attention following an auto accident. From a health perspective, it ensures that all injuries, apparent or not, are professionally assessed and treated. From a legal and insurance standpoint, it provides the necessary documentation to substantiate claims and secure appropriate compensation. Remember, your health and well-being should always be the priority, and securing medical documentation is a key role player in protecting your interests in any post-accident proceedings.

Navigating the aftermath of an auto accident can indeed be a daunting experience. However, your actions in those initial moments can determine the situation's outcome. Prioritizing safety should always be your first concern. Whether it's moving to a safe area, using hazard lights, or checking for injuries, these immediate actions can have a lasting impact on the safety of everyone involved.

Documenting the accident scene is equally prudent. You create a factual event record by taking comprehensive photos and gathering witness information. This documentation is invaluable and a valuable resource in any subsequent legal or insurance processes. Moreover, always appreciate the importance of seeking medical attention, regardless of how you feel immediately post-accident. Some injuries are not immediately apparent, and getting a professional evaluation is crucial for your health and for any insurance claims or legal actions that may follow.

Moving to the next chapter, we will explore the post-accident procedures in detail. This includes navigating insurance claims, understanding the legal implications, and managing the various challenges that often arise after an auto accident. Remember, being informed and prepared are your best tools for effectively handling the aftermath of an auto accident.

## Chapter 1: At the Scene of the Accident - Summary Checklist

**Immediate Steps After an Accident**:

- ☐ Safety first! Move to a safe area if possible.
- ☐ Turn on hazard lights to signal an emergency.
- ☐ Check for immediate dangers like fire or leaking fuel.

**Assessing Injuries**:

- ☐ Quickly check yourself for injuries.
- ☐ Assess the condition of passengers and other involved parties.
- ☐ Call 911 immediately if there are any injuries.

**Interacting with Other Parties Involved**:

- ☐ Exchange contact and insurance information with the other driver(s).
- ☐ Keep conversations factual and avoid discussing faults or details of the accident.
- ☐ Collect contact information from any witnesses.

**Documenting the Scene**:

- ☐ Take photographs from multiple angles, capturing all vehicles involved.
- ☐ Document specific damages to each car.
- ☐ Capture wider shots of the accident scene, including road conditions, traffic signs, and signals.
- ☐ If injuries are visible, photograph them carefully, respecting privacy and sensitivity.

**Cooperating with Law Enforcement**:

- ☐ Wait for the police to arrive and secure the scene.
- ☐ Provide a factual account of the accident to the police.
- ☐ Do not speculate or guess about unknown details.

☐ Request a copy of the police report for your records.

**Remember**: Your actions at the accident scene are critical. Stay calm, prioritize safety, and gather as much information as possible. These initial steps are crucial for any subsequent legal or insurance processes.

---

Don't miss out on our essential checklists! Click the QR code or visit https://www.pinderplotkin.com/crash-course-checklist to get your copy and stay prepared at every step of your auto accident journey.

# 2. POST-ACCIDENT PROCEDURES

Once the immediate safety and health concerns are addressed at the accident scene, the following steps involve navigating the post-accident process. This chapter will guide you through essential procedures to manage the aftermath effectively, protecting your health, legal rights, and financial interests.

## Seeking Medical Attention

After a car accident, adrenaline often surges, masking the pain and symptoms of injuries. This natural reaction can trick you into thinking you are unharmed. However, the absence of immediate pain or visible injuries does not guarantee that you are injury-free. As a result, seeking medical attention after a car accident is crucial, regardless of how you initially feel.

### Hidden Injuries and Delayed Symptoms

As mentioned previously, some injuries sustained in auto accidents are not immediately apparent. Conditions like whiplash, internal bleeding, concussions, or even some spinal injuries may not show symptoms for hours or even days after the accident. A medical professional is trained to identify these hidden injuries, ensuring that any underlying issues are promptly and appropriately addressed. Early diagnosis can prevent complications that might arise from untreated injuries and aids in a more efficient recovery process.

## Types of Unnoticeable Injuries Common in Auto Accidents

**Whiplash and Neck Injuries**: These often result from the sudden, jerking motion of the head, typical in rear-end collisions. Symptoms might include neck pain, stiffness, and headaches.

**Concussions**: As a form of traumatic brain injury, concussions can occur when the brain is jolted inside the skull. Symptoms can be subtle, such as confusion, dizziness, or difficulty concentrating.

**Broken Bones**: The impact of a collision can easily break or fracture bones. Some fractures might not be immediately painful or visible but can cause long-term issues if not treated.

**Soft Tissue Injuries**: These involve damage to muscles, ligaments, and tendons and might not be immediately evident due to adrenaline.

**Internal Injuries**: One of the most serious types, internal injuries, such as damage to organs or internal bleeding, might not show symptoms immediately but are life-threatening.

## Following Medical Advice

Following their advice and treatment plan is critical once a healthcare professional has evaluated your condition. Whether it's medication, physical therapy, rest, or follow-up appointments, adherence to medical advice not only aids in your recovery but also impacts any insurance or legal claims related to the accident. Disregarding medical advice or prematurely discontinuing treatment can be used against you in legal proceedings, potentially undermining the legitimacy of your claims.

### Documenting Your Medical Treatment

Documenting your medical treatment is as crucial as the treatment itself. Things to document include:

- **Medical Reports**: These provide an official record of your injuries and the initial evaluation following the accident.
- **Treatment Records**: Detailed records of all treatments, including dates, types of treatment, and medical providers' names.
- **Receipts and Bills**: Keep all receipts related to medical expenses, including medications, treatments, and equipment like braces or crutches.
- **Follow-up Care**: Document any follow-up visits, including what was discussed and any changes in your treatment plan.
- **Impact on Daily Life**: Keeping a personal log detailing how the injuries impact your daily activities and quality of life is beneficial.

These records play a vital role in insurance claims and legal proceedings. They provide a timeline of your injuries and treatment, substantiating your compensation claims. In the case of legal action, this documentation forms a part of the evidence, supporting your case and ensuring you receive fair compensation for your injuries and suffering.

Regardless of the severity, seeking medical attention promptly after an auto accident is crucial, even if you feel fine initially. The types of injuries from such incidents can vary widely, and some may not be immediately evident. Adhering to medical advice and meticulously documenting your treatment journey is essential to safeguarding your health and protecting your legal and insurance rights.

## Reporting the Accident to Your Insurance

Promptly reporting the accident to your insurance company is your next important step following any auto accident. When you contact them, it's important to relay the incident's details accurately but be mindful to steer clear of conjecture or admitting fault. Your description should be factual, sticking to what occurred without personal interpretation or assumption about who was at fault.

When communicating with your insurance provider, make sure to provide:

- **Basic Information**: Share the date and time of the accident, the location, and the contact details of all parties involved, including any witnesses.
- **Accident Details**: Describe the circumstances of the accident as objectively as possible. Include information about the road conditions, weather, and any immediate post-accident actions.
- **Photos and Documentation**: Provide any photographs or documentation from the accident scene, such as photos of the vehicles involved, damage incurred, and any relevant road signs or signals.
- **Police Report Reference**: If you or anyone else filed a police report, provide its reference number. This

report can offer an unbiased account of the accident and may be critical in the claims process.

Understanding your insurance policy is also critical for working through this process. Be aware of your coverage limits and deductibles. Inquire about the next steps, such as getting your vehicle appraised for damages or submitting additional documentation.

Expect the claims process to involve several steps, including an investigation by the insurance company, an assessment of vehicle damage, and potential discussions about settlement for any damages or injuries. Be prepared for this process to take time, and maintain open communication with your insurer throughout. Remember, your insurance company is there to guide you through this process, so don't hesitate to ask questions or seek clarifications as needed.

### Documenting Everything

Meticulous documentation is key in the aftermath of an auto accident. Maintaining a comprehensive record of all documents related to the accident not only aids in streamlining the insurance claim process but is also incredibly valuable if any legal action should arise. This includes gathering and organizing medical and police reports, correspondence with insurance companies, and other pertinent documents.

Here are some tips for effectively organizing and maintaining these records:

- **Create a Dedicated File**: Establish a dedicated file or folder, either digital or physical, specifically for accident-related documents. This centralizes all information, making it easy to access and reference.

- **Chronological Organization**: Arrange documents in chronological order. This helps create a clear timeline of events, treatments, and communications.
- **Secure Digital Copies**: Scan or take clear photographs of all documents to create digital copies. Store these in a secure cloud service or on an external drive as a backup.
- **Detailed Medical Records:** Include all medical reports, treatment details, prescriptions, and bills. Document any diagnoses, treatment plans, and follow-up care.
- **Accurate Police Reports:** Secure a copy of the police report. This report is an unbiased account of the accident and can be crucial for insurance and legal proceedings.
- **Insurance Correspondence**: Keep copies of all interactions with your insurance company. This includes emails, letters, and notes from phone conversations detailing dates, times, and the names of the representatives you spoke with.
- **Expense Records**: Document all expenses related to the accident, such as medical bills, travel costs to medical appointments, and repair costs for vehicle damage.
- **Regular Updates**: Continually update your documentation with any new treatments, communications, or other relevant information.

Organized and thorough documentation ensures that you have all the necessary information at your fingertips, which can expedite the insurance claims process and provide essential evidence in case of legal proceedings. It's crucial to protect your rights and interests after an auto accident.

## Understanding Your Insurance Coverage

In the aftermath of an accident, navigating the intricacies of your auto insurance policy is essential. Understanding the specifics of your coverage can significantly influence how you handle claims and negotiations with insurance adjusters. This comprehensive overview aims to demystify standard insurance terms and coverages, guiding you through the process of making informed decisions based on your policy.

### Liability Coverage

Liability insurance is a fundamental component of auto insurance policies. It covers damages for which you might be legally responsible, including bodily injury and property damage to others. There are typically two components, bodily injury liability and property damage liability:

- **Bodily Injury Liability**: This covers medical expenses, lost wages, and legal fees if you are found responsible for injuring someone in an auto accident.
- **Property Damage Liability**: This covers the cost of repairs for damage caused to someone else's property, such as their vehicle, fence, or building.

**Collision Coverage**: Collision coverage is designed to cover the cost of repairs to your vehicle after an accident, regardless of who is at fault. It's imperative if your car is newer or has high value. Collision coverage usually requires you to pay a deductible before the insurance company pays for the remaining repair costs.

**Comprehensive Coverage**: Comprehensive insurance covers damages to your vehicle that are not caused by collisions. This includes scenarios such as theft, vandalism, natural disasters, and accidents with animals. Like collision coverage, it typically involves a deductible.

**Medical Payments Coverage / Personal Injury Protection (PIP)**: These coverages are designed to pay for medical expenses for you and your passengers after an accident. PIP, which is mandatory in some states, can also cover lost wages and other related expenses, regardless of who is at fault.

**Uninsured/Underinsured Motorist Coverage**: This coverage protects you if you're in an accident with a driver who either lacks insurance or has insufficient insurance to cover your damages. It can cover both bodily injury and property damage.

**PRO TIP**:

In cases where you possess only collision coverage and find yourself in an accident with an uninsured at-fault driver, be aware that your insurance policy might not readily inform you about the option to file an uninsured property damage claim, which often comes with a lower deductible. The application of this coverage is governed by state law, so it's wise to consult with an attorney. Insurance companies typically require proof that the other driver was uninsured (like a denial letter) before they'll transfer your claim to the uninsured property damage department. This subtle requirement is a tactic that saves insurers millions annually.

### Understanding Policy Limits

Each coverage type in your insurance policy has its own limits, which are the maximum amounts your insurance company will pay in case of a claim. Understanding these limits is crucial as they directly affect how much coverage you have available in various situations.

**Deductibles**: A deductible is the amount you agree to pay out of pocket before your insurance coverage kicks in. Higher deductibles generally lower your premium costs but mean more out-of-pocket expenses when you file a claim.

**Exclusions**: Every insurance policy has exclusions – specific situations or types of damage that are not covered. Understanding these is crucial, as it helps you identify any gaps in your coverage that you might need to address.

### How to Review Your Policy

**Read the Declarations Page**: This summarizes your policy, including your coverages, policy limits, and deductibles. Review it carefully to understand the basics of your policy.

**Understand the Policy Wording**: Insurance policies can be complex. Don't hesitate to contact your insurance agent to explain any terms or conditions you don't understand.

**Check for Updates**: Make sure your policy reflects your current situation or any changes in your life, such as moving to a new address, buying a new car, or changing your driving record, which can affect your coverage needs.

**Know Your Rights and Responsibilities**: Understand what is required of you when you file a claim, such as prompt reporting of accidents and cooperation with the insurance company.

**PRO TIP**:

Remember, insurance adjusters work for the insurance company, and their primary goal is to settle claims for as little as possible. Therefore, knowing the specifics of your policy empowers you to advocate for a fair settlement that adequately covers your losses.

## Negotiating with the Insurance Adjuster

When you are armed with knowledge about your policy, you can negotiate with insurance adjusters more effectively. Understanding your coverages and their limits helps you evaluate whether the settlement offers made by the insurance company are fair and in line with your policy terms.

Understanding your auto insurance policy is one of the few vital aspects of effectively managing the aftermath of an auto accident. It equips you with the knowledge necessary to navigate claims, negotiate with adjusters, and ensure that you receive the compensation you're entitled to under your policy. Regular reviews and updates of your policy, along with a clear understanding of its terms, can significantly ease the process of dealing with insurance claims following an accident. Remember, your insurance policy is a contract between you and your insurer, and being well-informed about its details is key to upholding your end of the agreement while ensuring your rights are protected.

## Dealing with Other Party's Insurance

Navigating communications with the other party's insurance company after an auto accident can be challenging post-accident. These companies are often quick to make contact in an attempt to resolve the matter swiftly, but it's crucial to approach these interactions with a strategic mindset.

The primary goal of the other party's insurance company is to minimize their financial liability. When they contact you, it's typically to gather information that could be used to dispute your claim or reduce the amount they pay. **It's important to remember that you are under no obligation to provide them with any information beyond basic contact details.**

### Communicating with Other Insurance Companies

**Initial Contact**: Stay calm and collected if the other party's insurer contacts you. Provide only your basic personal information. Avoid discussing details of the accident or your injuries. You may be concussed or under the influence of medication.

**Avoid Recorded Statements:** Insurance adjusters may ask for a recorded statement. Politely decline to provide one until you have consulted with an attorney. What you say can be used against you in your claim. This also applies if your insurance company requires a recorded statement.

**Settlement Offers:** Be wary of early settlement offers. These are often made before the full extent of your injuries; damages are known and can be significantly lower than what you're entitled to. Accepting such an offer usually means waiving your right to seek additional compensation later.

**Consult an Attorney:** Before engaging in detailed discussions or negotiations with the other party's insurance, it's advisable to consult with a personal injury attorney. They can provide valuable guidance on what information to share and what to withhold.

**Document Interactions:** Keep detailed records of all interactions with the other party's insurance company. Note the date, time, the name of the person you spoke with, and the conversation details.

**Understand Your Rights:** Familiarize yourself with your rights. You are not required to accept an offer or provide detailed information about your injuries or damages.

## Tips for Effective Communication

**Be Clear and Concise**: Respond clearly and concisely when communicating with the insurer. Stick to factual information.

**Do Not Speculate**: Avoid speculating about fault, your injuries, or other aspects of the accident. Speculation can be misconstrued and used to undermine your claim.

**Seek Clarification**: If you don't understand a question or a term used, ask for clarification. You have the right to understand all aspects of the conversation fully.

**Know When to Step Back**: If you feel pressured or uncertain during a conversation, it's okay to step back and say that you will continue the discussion later, preferably after consulting with an attorney.

**The Role of Legal Representation**: Having legal representation can be invaluable in dealing with the other party's insurance company. An experienced attorney can handle communications on your behalf, ensuring that your rights are protected. They can also evaluate settlement offers, negotiate more effectively, and work to secure the compensation you deserve based on the details of your case.

Dealing with the other party's insurance company requires a balance of cautious communication and understanding of your legal rights. It's essential to remember that these companies are not working in your favor. Protecting your interests, whether through careful communication or by enlisting the help of an attorney, is crucial in ensuring a fair outcome for your insurance claim following an auto accident.

**PRO TIP:**

Engaging an attorney usually brings more advantages than the cost of their contingency fee, which importantly, doesn't require any upfront payment and is only applicable if the attorney successfully recovers funds for you. In my experience, every interaction a person has with the opposing driver's insurance company tends to diminish the value of their claim.

### Considering Legal Representation

You will reach a pivotal moment after an auto accident - the decision to seek legal representation. A personal injury attorney can be invaluable in such situations, offering expert advice and acting as a robust advocate for your interests.

### When to Strongly Consider Hiring an Attorney vs. Self-Help

**Serious Injuries or Significant Damages**: If the accident resulted in substantial injuries or significant property damage, legal guidance is crucial. An attorney can help you accurately assess your claim's value, including the long-term effects of injuries.

**Disputed Fault**: In accidents where the fault is not clear or if it's being disputed, an attorney can help protect your rights. They can gather evidence to support your version of events and work to establish liability.

**PRO TIP**:

We've often taken on cases where we've had to deal with correspondence and medical authorizations our clients have already sent to insurance companies. Regrettably, these actions have sometimes severely compromised their claims. In states with Contributory Negligence laws, even minimal fault (as little as 0.1%) in an accident can nullify your chance of recovery. Insurance companies are particularly keen on receiving detailed accounts from claimants without legal representation. Those impulsive, late-night emails expressing your frustration can significantly harm your case, if it's still viable. They also signal to adjusters that you might struggle under the pressure of a trial, potentially making you an ineffective witness, difficult for a jury to sympathize with. Moreover, be mindful that any correspondence you send could be read in court by the judge or jury.

**Complex Legal Situations**: In certain scenarios, such as accidents involving commercial vehicles, uninsured drivers, or multiple parties, an attorney's expertise can be essential in navigating those complexities.

**Insurance Company Challenges**: If you're facing challenges from insurance companies, such as denied claims or low settlement offers, an attorney can negotiate on your behalf and fight for a fair settlement.

## Why Hiring an Attorney is Beneficial

**Expertise in Law and Procedures**: Personal injury attorneys bring a deep understanding of legal procedures and can handle the legal aspects of your claim, allowing you to focus on recovery.

**Negotiation Skills**: Attorneys are skilled negotiators who can deal with insurance companies effectively, often securing higher settlements than individuals can achieve independently.

**Resource for Legal Advice**: They can offer tailored advice on the merits of your case, helping you make informed decisions.

**Litigation Support**: If your case goes to court, an attorney will represent you throughout the process, advocating on your behalf and working to secure the best possible outcome.

While not every auto accident requires legal representation, consulting with a personal injury attorney can provide clarity and direction, particularly in complex or severe cases. Their expertise not only aids in navigating the legal and insurance landscapes but ensures that your rights are adequately protected throughout the claim process.

## Managing Financial Implications

An auto accident often triggers a cascade of financial responsibilities that can be overwhelming. From immediate medical expenses to the long-term costs of vehicle repairs and possible income loss, understanding how to manage these financial implications is crucial for your stability and recovery.

### Addressing Immediate Costs

**Understanding Insurance Coverage**: Your first line of financial defense is often your auto insurance policy. Familiarize yourself with the terms of your coverage, especially aspects like Personal Injury Protection (PIP) or Medical Payments (Med-Pay), which can provide immediate relief for medical expenses, irrespective of fault.

**Health Insurance**: Don't overlook your health insurance policy. It might cover a significant portion of your medical bills post-accident. Be aware of any deductibles or copayments that you are responsible for and how they integrate with your auto insurance.

### Securing Compensation

**Insurance Claims**: If another driver is at fault, filing a claim against their insurance is a viable option. This claim can cover various costs, from vehicle repairs to medical bills. Ensure you have a clear understanding of what their policy covers.

**Legal Recourse**: When insurance coverage is insufficient, or liability is disputed, seeking legal advice may be necessary. A lawyer can guide you in pursuing a settlement or court action to recover costs not covered by insurance.

### Long-term Financial Management

**Post-Accident Budget**: Post-accident financial planning involves careful budgeting. It may require adjusting your spending to accommodate new expenses or reduced income, especially if your injuries impact your ability to work.

**Explore Financial Assistance**: Investigate if you are eligible for any financial assistance programs, particularly if the accident results in long-term disability or unemployment. These programs can provide vital support during your recovery period. Note: some programs will subrogate - meaning they expect the benefits to be repaid by you from settlement money or judgments you obtain.

**Professional Financial Advice**: Consult with a financial advisor or attorney can be beneficial. They can help you understand the full scope of your financial options and guide you in managing insurance claims and legal settlements.

## Navigating Insurance Claims

**Comprehensive Documentation**: Keeping meticulous records of all your accident-related expenses is critical. This includes medical bills, repair receipts, and records of lost wages. Accurate documentation will strengthen your insurance claims and any legal cases.

**Effective Communication with Insurers**: Open and ongoing communication with your insurance company is essential. Provide them with comprehensive documentation to facilitate the claims process. Be prepared for negotiations and understand your policy's limits and exclusions.

## Understanding Legal Settlements

**Evaluate Offers**: Consider a settlement offer carefully if you are presented with it. Assess whether it covers all your expenses and lost income, both immediate and future. Sometimes, initial offers may not fully account for long-term rehabilitation or chronic conditions that might arise.

**Legal Representation**: A personal injury attorney can be instrumental in evaluating settlement offers. Their expertise can be critical in negotiations, ensuring you receive fair compensation that aligns with the accident's impact on your life.

Financial management in the wake of an auto accident encompasses understanding and utilizing your insurance coverages, effectively documenting all expenses, and exploring all avenues for compensation. Balancing immediate needs with long-term financial implications requires careful planning and, often, professional guidance. Whether through insurance negotiations or legal settlements, your aim should be to secure a financial footing that supports your recovery and compensates for any losses or damages incurred. Proactive and informed financial management is key to navigating the post-accident landscape.

## Chapter 2: Post-Accident Procedures - Summary Checklist

**Seeking Medical Attention**:

- ☐ Seek medical attention to check for hidden injuries immediately, even if you don't feel injured.
- ☐ Follow through with all recommended treatments and attend follow-up appointments.

**Reporting the Accident to Your Insurance**:

- ☐ Report the accident to your insurance company promptly.
- ☐ Provide concise, factual details about the accident but avoid admitting fault or speculating about the cause.

**Dealing with the Other Party's Insurance:**

- ☐ Avoid leaving the accident scene until it is appropriate to do so.
- ☐ Do not admit fault or liability at the scene; stick to the facts when speaking to others involved or the police.
- ☐ Resist the urge to immediately agree to settlement offers without understanding the full extent of damages or consulting with a professional.
- ☐ Don't neglect to document the accident scene and collect witness information.

These steps are crucial in the aftermath of an auto accident. They ensure your safety, protect your rights, and set the foundation for any necessary insurance claims or legal actions. Staying informed and cautious during each stage of post-accident procedures can significantly impact the ease and success of your recovery process.

---

Don't miss out on our essential checklists! Click the QR code or visit https://www.pinderplotkin.com/crash-course-checklist to get your copy and stay prepared at every step of your auto accident journey.

# 3. LEGAL ASPECTS OF AUTO ACCIDENTS

The resulting aftermath of an auto accident involves more than addressing physical injuries or dealing with insurance companies; it often requires understanding the complex web of legal implications. This chapter is designed to illuminate the legal aspects of auto accidents, providing you clarity on fault, liability, state laws, and the intricacies of dealing with insurance claims and potential litigation. I aim to demystify these processes and empower you with knowledge to protect your rights and interests.

## Understanding Fault and Liability

In the realm of auto accidents, the concept of fault is central to resolving claims and determining liability. Fault refers to who was responsible for causing the accident, and its determination is a critical factor in the legal and insurance processes following an incident.

### Exploring the Concept of Fault

In auto accidents, the fault is typically centered around the idea of negligence – a failure to behave with the level of care that someone of ordinary prudence would have exercised under the same circumstances. This includes actions like disobeying traffic laws, driving distractedly, or failing to signal while turning. Determining possible negligence is crucial since it directly impacts the outcome of insurance claims and legal proceedings.

In many jurisdictions, concepts like contributory and comparative negligence come into play and are two terms you will want in your tool belt early in the process. These principles involve assessing the degree of fault of each party involved in an accident. For instance, in a case where a driver was speeding, and another made an unsafe lane change, both may be found partially at fault.

**Contributory Negligence**: The contributory negligence doctrine bars plaintiffs from collecting damages if they are found partially at fault for their accident-related injuries.

**Comparative Negligence**: The plaintiff is not barred from collecting damages if they are found partially at fault for their accident-related injuries, whereas the comparative negligence doctrine does not.

**To illustrate the difference, consider these scenarios:**

Imagine a situation where two drivers, Alice and Bob, are involved in a car accident at an intersection. Alice was speeding, going 15 miles over the speed limit. Bob ran a red light just before the collision. Both drivers contributed to the accident in this scenario: Alice was speeding, and Bob was running a red light.

Under a contributory negligence system, if a party is even slightly negligent (i.e., contributed in any way to the accident), they cannot recover damages.

In a state that follows strict contributory negligence rules, if Alice tries to claim damages for her car from Bob, her claim would be barred entirely because she was also negligent (speeding). The same would apply to Bob if he tried to claim damages from Alice.

Comparative negligence, on the other hand, allocates fault between the parties involved in an accident. Each party is responsible for their percentage of fault. If Alice is found to be 40% at fault for speeding and Bob 60% at fault for running a red light, then Alice can recover 60% of her damages from Bob, and Bob can recover 40% of his damages from Alice.

In a contributory negligence system, any fault on the part of the plaintiff can bar recovery completely. In a comparative negligence system, recovery is still possible but is reduced by the plaintiff's percentage of fault, with specific rules varying depending on whether it's a pure or modified system.

States like Virginia and Maryland may follow these principles differently. In some states, if you are found even slightly at fault, you might be unable to collect any compensation (contributory negligence). In contrast, in others, your compensation may be reduced by your percentage of fault (comparative negligence). Some states don't view speeding as contributory negligence - this is no universal guidebook for the rules of the road.

## Determining Liability

Liability determination is a systematic process conducted by insurance companies and law enforcement. It involves collecting and analyzing various pieces of evidence – including photos from the accident scene, surveillance footage, vehicle damage, witness statements, and police reports. This information helps establish a clear picture of the events leading up to the accident and who bears the responsibility.

Insurance companies evaluate this evidence alongside any relevant laws to determine liability and the extent of damages to be compensated. Therefore, this evidence's accuracy and comprehensiveness are crucial in effectively determining fault and liability.

Understanding these elements of fault and liability can significantly impact how you approach your post-accident actions and decisions. Knowing how fault is established, the nuances of contributory and comparative negligence, and the process of determining liability can guide you in navigating the often complex aftermath of an auto accident.

**State Laws and Regulations**

Each state has its unique set of laws that can significantly influence the outcome of your case. Therefore, your success relies on a firm understanding of state-specific regulations and how they affect your rights and responsibilities in the event of an auto accident.

**Auto Accident Laws and Variations**

Just like states have differing laws on the road, laws related to auto accidents can vary widely from state to state. For instance, some states operate under 'no-fault' rules, where your insurance coverage pays for your damages regardless of who caused the accident. In contrast, others follow a more traditional fault-based system. Additionally, Personal Injury Protection (PIP) requirements variations can affect how medical expenses and lost wages are covered post-accident.

Awareness of these nuances is essential, as they directly impact your insurance claims and potential compensation.

### Statute of Limitations

The statute of limitations sets a deadline for filing a lawsuit, which can vary depending on the state. You must meet this deadline to pursue legal action to seek compensation. For example, the timeframe in one state might be two years from the accident date, while another might offer three. This variation underscores the importance of consulting with legal counsel soon after your accident to ensure you adhere to these time-sensitive requirements.

### State-Specific Insurance Requirements

Understanding the minimum insurance coverage required in your state is also crucial. For instance, Virginia and Maryland have specific minimum coverage requirements that all drivers must meet. These requirements play a significant role in the insurance claims process and can affect the compensation you may receive after an accident.

Being well-informed about your state's specific auto accident laws, the statute of limitations, and insurance requirements are critical players in this process. Understanding these concepts helps you make informed decisions post-accident and ensures you are adequately prepared to protect your rights and interests after an auto accident.

### The Role of Police Reports in Your Claim

As we mentioned previously, a police report becomes an indispensable document in the aftermath of an auto accident. It plays a pivotal role in both insurance claims and legal proceedings. This report provides an unbiased account of the accident, often determining the direction of insurance negotiations and the outcomes of legal claims.

### Significance in Insurance and Legal Matters

Police reports contain crucial details such as the accident's time, location, circumstances, and observations on damages, injuries, and potential law violations. These details are fundamental in establishing fault and liability. For instance, if a report indicates that one party violated traffic laws, it significantly influences the fault determination, thereby affecting insurance claims and potential lawsuits.

### Addressing Inconsistencies

Sometimes, police reports may contain discrepancies or inaccuracies. It's important to review the report thoroughly upon receiving it. If you find errors or missing information, these can often be challenged or supplemented with additional evidence such as witness statements, photographs of the scene, or expert testimonies.

### Obtaining the Police Report

**To acquire a copy of the police report, follow these steps:**

**Identify the Relevant Department**: Determine which law enforcement agency responded to the accident – it could be local police, county sheriff, or state troopers.

**Request Procedure**: Contact the department for their specific process for requesting a police report. This information is often available on their website as well.

**Provide Necessary Information**: You may need to provide details such as the date of the accident, location, names of involved parties, and the incident number, if available.

**Understand the Waiting Period**: Be aware that a waiting period might occur before the report is available. This can vary from a few days to a couple of weeks.

**Pay Any Required Fees**: Some departments may charge a fee for the report. Ensure you are aware of and have the means to pay this fee.

Proactively obtaining the report and addressing any issues it may contain is vital in safeguarding your interests. It not only aids in insurance claims and legal actions but serves as a key piece of evidence in establishing the facts surrounding the accident.

## Navigating Insurance Claims and Adjusters

You can employ several effective strategies when dealing with insurance adjusters after an auto accident. Understanding this process to the best of your ability will help ensure that you receive fair compensation for your damages and injuries, as you deserve.

### The Insurance Claims Process

**Initiate the Claim**: Contact your insurance company immediately after the accident to initiate the claim. Provide a detailed account of the incident, sticking to factual information.

**Documentation**: Gather and organize all relevant documents, including police reports, medical records, photographs of the scene, and any receipts related to the accident (such as repair costs and medical expenses). This documentation will support your claim.

**Communication**: Keep a record of all communications with your insurance company. This includes dates of conversations, the names of representatives you speak with, and details of what was discussed.

**Understand the Timeframes**: Inquire about the timeline for processing your claim. Insurance companies typically have set timeframes, but these can vary based on the complexity of your case.

### Dealing with Insurance Adjusters

**Effective Communication**: When speaking with insurance adjusters, be clear and concise. Stick to the facts of the case and avoid sharing unnecessary personal opinions or details.

**Evaluate Settlement Offers**: Carefully review any settlement offers. Ensure they adequately cover all your expenses and losses related to the accident. If an offer seems too low, don't feel pressured to accept it immediately.

**Negotiation:** Be prepared to negotiate. Present your evidence effectively to justify why you deserve a higher settlement.

### Disputing Insurance Decisions

**Understanding the Grounds for Dispute**: If you believe the insurance company's decision is unfair or fails to cover your expenses adequately, identify specific reasons for your dispute. This could be due to an undervaluation of damages or an incorrect interpretation of policy terms. This is another pivotal example in which I strongly recommend that you consult an attorney.

**File a Dispute**: Follow the insurance company's dispute filing procedure. This often involves submitting a formal letter outlining your case and providing supporting evidence.

**See External Review**: If the dispute is not resolved satisfactorily, you may seek an external review. This can involve contacting state insurance regulators or pursuing legal action.

Working through and with insurance claims and adjusters requires a combination of organization, effective communication, and a willingness to stand firm on your needs. Being well-prepared with documentation and clearly understanding your policy will strengthen your position. Remember, while the goal is to reach a fair settlement, you have the right to challenge decisions that do not adequately compensate you for your losses.

### Legal Representation: When and Why

The aftermath of an auto accident can sometimes require more than just dealing with insurance companies; it may necessitate legal expertise. You need to understand when and why you should engage in legal representation, which is essential in safeguarding your interests and ensuring a fair outcome.

## Benefits of Legal Representation

**Expert Negotiation:** Lawyers are skilled in negotiation, often securing higher settlements from insurance companies than individuals can achieve independently.

**Legal Systems Expertise**: Attorneys are adept at navigating the complexities of the legal system, including court procedures, filing deadlines, and legal documentation.

**Advocacy**: Your attorney acts as your advocate, representing your best interests throughout the process. They provide objective advice and guide you in making informed decisions.

## Choosing the Right Attorney

When considering hiring an attorney, use the following criteria:

**Experience**: Look for an attorney with experience handling auto accident cases like yours. Experience in this specific area of law is vital for effective representation.

**Track Record**: Inquire about the attorney's track record in handling auto accident cases, particularly those that have gone to trial or resulted in substantial settlements.

**Client Testimonials**: Client feedback can provide insights into an attorney's performance and client service. Positive testimonials can be a good indicator of an attorney's effectiveness and client satisfaction.

**Communication Skills**: Choose an attorney who communicates clearly and keeps you informed throughout the process. A good lawyer should be accessible and responsive to your questions and concerns.

**Compatibility**: It's important that you feel comfortable with your attorney. A good rapport can make the process less stressful and more productive.

## Contingency Fees

In addition to understanding when and why to hire an attorney, it's equally important to comprehend the financial aspect of legal representation, particularly the contingency fee arrangement. This payment structure is commonly used in auto accident cases and can significantly influence your decision to hire an attorney.

Under a contingency fee arrangement, the attorney agrees to represent you without requiring any upfront payment. Instead, their fee is contingent upon winning the case or securing a settlement for you. The fee is typically a predetermined percentage of the settlement amount or court award. This percentage can vary but usually ranges from 33% (1/3rd) to 40%, depending on the complexity of the case and the attorney's policies. Dog bites and slip-and-falls tend to have increased percentages in certain States where insurance companies have lobbied for insurance-friendly laws.

The key advantage of this arrangement is that it reduces the financial risk for you as a client. You do not owe them any legal fees if the attorney does not win the case or obtain a settlement. This setup aligns the attorney's interests with yours, as their payment directly depends on the success of your case.

However, I urge you to have a crystal-clear understanding of the contingency fee agreement before signing. Know exactly what the percentage covers and any potential additional costs, such as filing fees or costs for expert witnesses, that might not be included in the contingency fee.

Legal representation in auto accident cases is only sometimes necessary, but in most situations, it becomes crucial. A competent attorney can level the playing field, especially when dealing with complex cases, significant damages, or contentious fault disputes. They not only advocate on your behalf but also bring a wealth of knowledge and resources that can significantly impact the outcome of your case. The contingency fee arrangement makes legal representation more accessible, especially for those who can't afford to pay an attorney upfront. It allows individuals to seek justice and fair compensation without the burden of immediate legal fees, guaranteeing that legal assistance is available based on the case's merits rather than one's financial capacity. Researching and choosing the right attorney for your situation is critical to ensuring a fair resolution to your auto accident claim.

## Chapter 3: Legal Aspects of Auto Accidents - Summary Checklist

**Understanding Fault and Liability**:

- ☐ Review how fault is determined in your accident scenario.
- ☐ Understand the concept of negligence and how it applies to your case.
- ☐ Familiarize yourself with contributory and comparative negligence principles.

**State Laws and Regulations that Impact Your Case**:

- ☐ Research and understand the specific auto accident laws in your state.
- ☐ Note the statute of limitations in your state for filing a lawsuit.
- ☐ Be aware of your state's specific insurance requirements and how they affect your claim.

**The Role of Police Reports in Your Claim**:

- ☐ Obtain a copy of the police report as soon as it's available.
- ☐ Review the report for accuracy and completeness.
- ☐ Understand how the report's details impact fault determination and liability.

**Navigating Insurance Claims and Adjusters**:

- ☐ Initiate an insurance claim promptly after the accident.
- ☐ Organize all relevant documents and evidence to support your claim.
- ☐ Communicate effectively with insurance adjusters, avoiding admissions of fault.
- ☐ Be prepared to negotiate settlement offers.

**Legal Representation: When and Why**:

- ☐ Assess the benefit of hiring an attorney.
- ☐ Research potential attorneys focusing on their experience in auto accident cases.

**Contingency Fees**:

- ☐ Understand the contingency fee arrangement if considering hiring an attorney.
- ☐ Clarify with your attorney what the contingency fee covers and any additional costs.
- ☐ Evaluate the financial implications of a contingency fee agreement on your potential settlement or award.

This checklist serves as a guide through the critical legal aspects of an auto accident. From understanding fault and navigating state laws to effectively dealing with insurance claims and considering legal representation, each step is a pivotal movement toward a fair resolution of your case. Remember, being informed and proactive about these legal aspects can significantly impact the outcome of your post-accident proceedings.

---

Don't miss out on our essential checklists! Click the QR code or visit https://www.pinderplotkin.com/crash-course-checklist to get your copy and stay prepared at every step of your auto accident journey.

# 4. MANAGING INJURIES AND MEDICAL ISSUES

As you know, experiencing an auto accident can have a profound impact on your physical and mental well-being. This chapter is dedicated to guiding you through the process of managing medical issues and injuries post-accident. I will explore common injuries, their treatment, and how to document them for insurance and legal purposes.

## Common Auto Accident Injuries

Tragically, auto accidents are prevalent and can lead to a wide array of injuries. These injuries vary in severity and can have immediate and lasting effects on an individual's life. Knowing the most common injuries sustained in auto accidents is crucial for immediate medical care and their long-term implications, whether for health, insurance claims, or legal proceedings. I find that people most often suffer from the following:

**Whiplash**: Perhaps the most well-known injury associated with car accidents, especially rear-end collisions, is whiplash, when the head is suddenly jerked forward and backward. This can strain the neck muscles and ligaments, leading to symptoms like neck pain and stiffness, headaches, dizziness, and sometimes fatigue. The psychological impact, including irritability and sleep disturbances, can also be significant.

**Concussions and Traumatic Brain Injuries (TBIs)**: Concussions, a mild form of TBI, occur when the brain is jolted inside the skull due to a sudden impact. Symptoms can range from headaches, confusion, and blurred vision to memory problems. More severe TBIs can lead to long-term cognitive issues, emotional distress, and even permanent brain damage.

**Bone Fractures**: The force of a car accident can easily fracture bones. Common fracture sites include the ribs, arms, legs, and pelvis. Severe fractures may require surgical intervention and can lead to chronic pain or mobility issues, significantly impacting daily life.

**Soft Tissue Injuries**: These injuries affect the body's soft tissues, including muscles, ligaments, and tendons. They manifest as pain, swelling, bruising, and reduced mobility. Common examples are sprains, strains, and contusions.

**Spinal Cord Injuries**: Spinal injuries can range from herniated discs and whiplash-related injuries to more severe spinal cord damage, potentially leading to partial or complete paralysis. Symptoms include pain, numbness, and, in severe cases, loss of limb function.

**Internal Injuries**: Internal injuries, such as internal bleeding or damage to internal organs, are particularly perilous because they may not present immediate symptoms. They can be life-threatening and often require swift medical intervention.

**Lacerations and Bruises**: Sharp objects like glass or metal can cause cuts or lacerations, while the impact can lead to significant bruising. These injuries can range from superficial skin wounds to deep tissue damage.

**Psychological Trauma**: Mental health conditions like post-traumatic stress disorder (PTSD), anxiety, and depression are common after experiencing a traumatic event like a car accident. These conditions can profoundly affect an individual's daily functioning and quality of life.

**Burn Injuries**: In cases where a vehicle catches fire post-collision or due to friction, occupants can suffer from burn injuries. These can range from minor superficial burns to severe third-degree burns requiring extensive medical treatment.

**Knee Trauma**: The sudden impact of a collision can cause the knees to hit the dashboard or seats, leading to injuries like anterior cruciate ligament (ACL) injuries or shattered kneecaps.

**Shoulder Injuries**: Shoulder injuries, including dislocations and rotator cuff injuries, are common, especially when the shoulder absorbs the impact in a collision.

**Chest Injuries**: Chest injuries, often caused by seat belts during a high-impact crash, can range from bruising or contusions to more severe injuries like broken ribs and internal injuries.

## Immediate and Long-Term Symptoms

**Immediate Symptoms**: Some injuries, like fractures, lacerations, and certain types of internal injuries, present immediate symptoms such as pain, visible bruising, or swelling. See to it the person receives immediate medical attention for these symptoms to prevent further complications.

**Delayed Symptoms**: Injuries like whiplash, concussions, or internal bleeding might not present symptoms immediately. This delay can be due to adrenaline and shock masking the pain. It's imperative to closely monitor one's health post-accident and seek medical attention if new symptoms develop.

**Psychological Impacts**: The emotional and psychological impacts of an auto accident, such as anxiety or PTSD, might take time to manifest. Mental health support is just as important as treating physical injuries.

**Long-Term Effects**: Certain injuries can have long-lasting effects, ranging from chronic pain and ongoing mobility issues to permanent disabilities or cognitive impairments. Continuous medical care, rehabilitation, and mental health support can be integral to managing these long-term challenges.

Auto accidents can result in a diverse range of injuries, each with its own set of challenges and required treatments. Recognizing the signs and symptoms – both immediate and delayed – is essential for timely and effective medical care. Moreover, understanding these injuries is highly valuable when navigating the complexities of insurance claims and legal proceedings post-accident. Remember, healing from an auto accident is a multidimensional process that encompasses not just physical recovery but also addresses the emotional and psychological aftermath. Comprehensive care, patience, and support are incredibly beneficial for recovery.

### Seeking Immediate Medical Attention

In the chaotic aftermath of an accident, adrenaline, and shock can often mask the pain and severity of injuries, leading some to believe they are unharmed mistakenly. We must emphasize the urgency of seeking immediate medical care. In the chaotic aftermath of an accident, adrenaline and shock can often mask the pain and severity of injuries, leading some to believe they are unharmed mistakenly. Internal or brain-related injuries may not present immediate symptoms. Therefore, prompt medical evaluation ensures that hidden injuries are identified and treated early, hopefully preventing potential complications or long-term health issues.

Every aspect of the examination and treatment is documented in medical reports upon visiting a medical facility. As we've learned, these reports play a vital role beyond just healthcare; they are essential records for any insurance claims or legal proceedings that may follow. They provide an official account of your injuries, the treatment prescribed, and any recommendations for follow-up care.

Obtaining and securely storing copies of all medical reports, diagnoses, and prescriptions related to your visit is imperative. These documents serve as proof of the medical attention received as a direct result of the accident. They are instrumental in substantiating your claims, ensuring that you receive the appropriate compensation for medical expenses incurred due to the accident. Remember, your health is paramount, and maintaining thorough documentation of your medical care safeguards your rights and interests post-accident.

When choosing a medical provider following an auto accident, focusing on immediate healthcare needs and considering the long-term legal implications is essential. If your case progresses to legal action, the testimony of a medical provider can be pivotal. They must be capable of confidently stating, within a reasonable degree of medical certainty, that their injuries are related to the car accident.

This aspect of the process can be complex, and your attorney's role becomes crucial. An experienced attorney can help guide you through selecting a medical provider who is not only suitable for your medical needs but also experienced and willing to testify in court if required. Attorneys often have networks of professional contacts, including medical providers who have experience in legal proceedings and are familiar with the process of providing court testimony.

Collaborating with your attorney and medical provider ensures that all aspects of your case are handled with the necessary expertise. It assures that the medical testimony provided is both credible and legally sound, significantly reinforcing the validity of your claim. Therefore, while prioritizing your health and recovery, consider leveraging your attorney's expertise to make informed decisions about your medical care in the context of potential legal proceedings.

## Follow-Up Care and Treatment

Post-accident recovery often extends beyond the initial medical treatment. Adhering to prescribed follow-up care and treatments is crucial to comprehensive recovery. It's essential for your physical healing and documenting the extent and progression of your injuries, which can be vital in any insurance claims or legal proceedings.

### Adhering to Medical Advice

An important part of determining a fair ruling is to follow the treatment plan laid out by your healthcare provider to the letter. This includes taking prescribed medications, attending physical therapy sessions if recommended, and going to all scheduled follow-up appointments. These appointments allow your healthcare provider to monitor your recovery, make necessary adjustments to your treatment, and document your progress. Skipping appointments or disregarding medical advice can hinder your recovery and impact the legitimacy of your insurance claims, as it could be misconstrued as a sign of a less serious injury.

### Consulting with Specialists

Depending on the nature and severity of your injuries, your primary care doctor may refer you to specialists. Orthopedists, for example, specialize in bone-related injuries, while neurologists deal with injuries to the nervous system, including any brain trauma. These specialists can provide more targeted treatments and offer expert insights into your recovery process. Seeking specialist care is important when symptoms persist or if you face complications, as they can offer advanced treatments and interventions that are crucial for your recovery journey.

Diligent follow-up care and treatment, including specialist consultations, when necessary, play a significant role in your overall recovery from an auto accident. They ensure the best possible physical recovery and provide comprehensive medical documentation that is essential for any related insurance or legal matters.

## Tracking your Medical Treatments, Records, and Expenses

**Organize Receipts**: Collect and organize all receipts related to your medical treatment. This includes doctor visits, medication costs, physical therapy sessions, and any necessary medical equipment.

**Travel Costs**: Remember to document travel expenses to and from medical appointments. This includes public transportation fares, gas receipts, or parking fees.

**Insurance Statements**: Keep copies of all correspondence with your insurance company, including statements and summaries of benefits used.

Maintaining these detailed records serves a dual purpose. It helps you and your healthcare providers understand the trajectory of your recovery and provides essential evidence in detailing the extent of your injuries and their impact on your life. This thorough documentation is invaluable in ensuring that you receive fair compensation for your injuries and the adjustments you've had to make to your lifestyle.

## Document the Recovery Process with a Detailed Medical Diary

Documenting your recovery process after an auto accident is essential to managing your health and any subsequent legal or insurance claims. A detailed record provides a tangible account of the accident's impact on your daily life and can be a powerful tool in supporting your claims. You'll want to record:

**Symptoms and Pain Levels**: Regularly jot down details about your symptoms and pain levels. Note any changes or patterns in your physical condition.

**Impact on Daily Activities**: Document how your injuries affect your daily activities. Include notes on any difficulties you encounter in performing regular tasks or any changes in your ability to work.

**Mood and Emotional Health**: Record any emotional or psychological effects you're experiencing. This can include changes in mood, sleep patterns, or anxiety levels.

**Rehabilitation Progress**: Keep track of your progress in physical therapy or other rehabilitation programs, noting improvements or challenges.

## The Role of Chiropractic Care, Physical Therapy, and Rehabilitation

Recovery after an auto accident often involves more than just immediate medical treatment; it extends into the realm of physical therapy and rehabilitation. These therapeutic processes play a crucial role in helping victims regain strength, mobility, and functionality, which can be impaired due to their injuries.

### Benefits of Physical Therapy

Physical therapy is an integral component of many post-accident treatment plans, offering a range of benefits:

**Restore Functionality**: Physical therapy aims to restore normal body function and mobility. Patients can gradually regain strength and flexibility in affected areas through targeted exercises and therapy techniques.

**Pain Management**: Therapists use various methods like massage, heat treatment, and specialized exercises to help manage and alleviate pain. This is especially beneficial for those wishing to avoid or minimize the use of pain medication.

**Prevent Long-term Damage**: Regular physical therapy can prevent the development of chronic issues or permanent damage following an injury. It encourages healing in a controlled, therapeutic manner.

**Customized Care**: Physical therapy programs are tailored to each patient's needs, considering their specific injuries and recovery goals.

**Incorporate Chiropractic Care**: For many accident victims, chiropractic care is a valuable addition to their rehabilitation regimen. Chiropractors can help realign the spine, relieve pain, and improve body mechanics, which is particularly beneficial for those who have suffered back or neck injuries.

## Document Your Progress

Maintaining accurate records of your physical therapy and chiropractic sessions is as vital as the therapy itself. These records should include:

**Dates and Details of Sessions**: Keep a log of each visit, noting the types of treatment received and the duration of each session.

**Progress Notes**: Document any progress or feedback from your therapists or chiropractors. This could include improvements in pain levels, increases in mobility, or milestones reached in your therapy.

**Home Exercises**: Record any exercises or activities recommended for you to do at home, along with your adherence and any observations about their impact.

**Response to Treatment**: Note how your body responds to various treatments. This can help in adjusting your therapy plan for optimal recovery.

Documenting your physical therapy and chiropractic care journey provides a detailed account of your efforts toward recovery and can be crucial in insurance and legal scenarios. It demonstrates the extent of your injuries and the ongoing efforts required for rehabilitation, which can be influential in securing adequate compensation for your injuries. It's a testament to the physical and emotional challenges faced during the recovery process and underscores the seriousness of your commitment to regaining your health and well-being.

### Understanding and Dealing with Trauma

The aftermath of an auto accident extends beyond physical injuries, often delving into the realm of emotional and psychological well-being. The trauma of such an event can evoke a multitude of emotional responses, affecting victims in profound and sometimes lasting ways. Understanding and addressing these impacts is as crucial as attending to physical health.

## Recognizing Emotional and Psychological Symptoms

Post-accident, individuals may experience a range of emotional and psychological reactions. Common symptoms include:

**Anxiety and Fear**: Feelings of anxiety or persistent fear, mainly related to or when driving or traveling in vehicles, are common. This can extend to general anxiety about daily activities or routines.

**Sleep Disturbances**: Difficulty sleeping, nightmares, or insomnia are often reported following an accident. This can lead to fatigue and exacerbate other symptoms.

**Mood Swings or Irritability**: Sudden mood changes or irritability, reduced tolerance for stress, and an overwhelming sense of frustration can occur.

**Depression**: Feelings of sadness, hopelessness, or a lack of interest in previously enjoyed activities can be signs of depression.

**Flashbacks and Intrusive Thoughts**: Re-experiencing the accident through flashbacks or having persistent intrusive thoughts about the event is a sign of post-traumatic stress.

**Physical Symptoms**: Psychological distress can manifest physically, leading to symptoms like headaches, nausea, or exacerbated pain from physical injuries.

## Seeking Professional Help

If you are experiencing any of these symptoms, consider seeking help from a mental health professional. Therapists, psychologists, and psychiatrists can provide support and treatment tailored to your specific needs. Therapies like cognitive-behavioral therapy (CBT) have proven effective in addressing anxiety and PTSD related to auto accidents. A few of the benefits of going to therapy include:

**Process the Trauma**: Therapy provides a safe space to process the accident and its impact on your life.

**Develop Coping Strategies**: Mental health professionals can equip you with strategies to manage anxiety, stress, and other symptoms.

**Address Co-Occurring Issues**: Often, pre-existing mental health conditions can be exacerbated by an accident. Therapy helps in addressing these issues comprehensively.

**Improve Quality of Life**: Effective therapy can significantly improve your overall quality of life post-accident.

### Strategies for Self-Care

In addition to professional help, numerous self-care strategies can aid in coping with emotional and psychological effects:

**Establish a Routine**: Try to maintain a daily routine to provide structure and normalcy.

**Stay Physically Active**: Engaging in physical activities can help reduce stress and improve mood.

**Healthy Eating and Sleeping Habits**: Prioritize a healthy diet and aim for regular sleep patterns.

**Mindfulness and Relaxation Techniques**: Practices like meditation, deep breathing, or yoga can effectively manage anxiety and stress.

**Social Support**: Lean on family, friends, or support groups. Sharing your experiences and feelings can be therapeutic.

**Journaling**: Writing about your thoughts and feelings can provide an outlet for expression and reflection.

### Long-term Emotional Care

While some symptoms may resolve relatively quickly, others might linger. Long-term emotional care is important. Regular check-ins with mental health professionals, continued self-care practices, and being aware of your emotional state are priorities in your post-auto accident recovery.

### Dealing with Stigma

There's often a stigma associated with seeking help for emotional or psychological issues. It's important to remember that seeking help is a sign of strength, not weakness. Addressing your mental health is an essential part of recovery.

### Impact on Daily Life

An auto accident's emotional and psychological effects can interfere with daily life, work, and relationships. Acknowledging and addressing these impacts is crucial. It's important to set realistic goals and give yourself time to heal.

### Support for Children and Adolescents

If children or adolescents are involved in an accident, be mindful of their emotional and psychological needs. Younger individuals may have different ways of expressing distress and may benefit from specialized child or adolescent therapy.

The emotional and psychological aftermath of an auto accident can be as significant as the physical impact. Acknowledging this and taking steps to address your mental health is crucial. Seeking professional help, employing self-care strategies, and understanding the importance of long-term care are all vital components of a holistic recovery process. Remember, healing is not just physical – it also encompasses your emotional and mental well-being.

### Preparing for the Long Haul

Navigating the aftermath of an auto accident often unfolds as a prolonged journey, marked by a series of steps and stages that require your attention and endurance. From continuous medical treatments to intricate insurance negotiations and the potential for legal proceedings, the path to recovery and resolution is rarely swift. Embracing patience and persistence is essential in this journey.

### Emphasize Patience and Persistence

The road to recovery can test your patience, especially when dealing with slow-healing injuries or protracted insurance claims. It's important to remember that recovery and legal processes follow their own timelines, which might be longer than anticipated. Persistence in following through with treatments, claims, and legal advice is crucial.

## Stay Organized

**Document Management**: Keep a detailed file of all documents related to the accident, including medical records, insurance communications, and legal correspondence. Organizing these documents chronologically can help you track the progression of your case and treatment.

**Calendar Management**: Use a calendar to keep track of medical appointments, legal consultations, and important deadlines. Setting reminders can help ensure that you don't miss critical appointments or due dates.

**Financial Planning**: Keep a ledger or spreadsheet to track expenses related to the accident, such as medical bills, repair costs, and any lost wages. This will be valuable for insurance claims and potential compensation.

## Maintain Focus

**Set Realistic Goals**: Set achievable goals for your recovery and legal process. Whether it's reaching a certain stage in your physical therapy or successfully filing all necessary insurance paperwork, small milestones can provide a sense of accomplishment.

**Seek Support**: Don't hesitate to lean on friends, family, or support groups for emotional and practical support. Having a strong support network can help you stay focused and motivated.

**Regular Updates**: Keep yourself informed about the status of your insurance claim and any legal proceedings. Regular check-ins with your attorney, doctor, or insurance agent can clearly show where things stand and what to expect next.

## Adapting to Changes

The journey post-accident may require you to adapt to changes in your physical abilities, lifestyle, or financial situation. Be open to making necessary adjustments and seek advice or counseling to help navigate these changes.

**Consult Experts**: Regular consultations with your medical providers, legal advisors, and financial experts can provide guidance and help you make informed decisions throughout the process.

The journey following an auto accident is often a marathon, not a sprint. It requires a combination of patience, organization, focus, and adaptability. You can navigate this challenging path by managing your documentation effectively, setting realistic goals, maintaining open lines of communication with professionals, and leaning on your support network. Remember, each step forward, no matter how small, is progress in your journey toward recovery and resolution.

## Document Treatment

**Keep Records**: Document all mental health appointments, treatments, and prescribed medications. This is important for tracking your recovery, insurance, and legal purposes.

**Insurance Claims**: Detailed mental health treatment records can support compensation claims, demonstrating the accident's impact on your overall well-being.

**Legal Proof**: In legal cases, documented evidence of mental health treatment can substantiate emotional and psychological damages claims.

Understanding and addressing the mental health fallout of an auto accident is as important as physical recovery. Professional help and thorough documentation are key components in managing these psychological responses, ensuring that your journey to recovery encompasses both your mental and physical health.

## Long-Term Health Consequences

Auto accidents can result in chronic pain and disabilities that might last long after the incident. Injuries like spinal damage or traumatic brain injuries can evolve into persistent health issues, necessitating long-term treatment and potentially leading to permanent disabilities. These conditions may require significant lifestyle adjustments, including modifications to living spaces, changes in employment, or reliance on long-term medical care.

Adjusting to life post-accident often involves redefining one's daily routine and work capacity. To navigate these changes effectively, seeking support through rehabilitation services, counseling, or support groups is important. Embracing adaptive strategies and seeking continual medical and psychological support will help you manage the lasting effects of severe auto accident injuries.

## Working with Insurance Companies

**DISCLAIMER:**

I recommend that you hire an attorney and do NOT correspond with the insurance company - especially if the accident occurred in a Contributory Negligence state: Alabama, Maryland, North Carolina, Virginia, and Washington D.C.

Navigating the realm of insurance claims post-auto accident can be challenging, especially when facing insurance adjusters trained to minimize payouts. These adjusters often use advanced AI algorithms and have access to a vast array of in-house attorneys, all geared toward devaluing claims. It's essential to approach this process with thorough preparation and an understanding of your rights.

### Submitting Medical Records

**Complete and Accurate Documentation**: Ensure all medical records submitted are complete and accurately reflect the treatments received. This includes detailed doctor reports, test results, and records of ongoing treatments.

**Organized Submission**: Organize your documents chronologically and clearly label them. This helps the adjuster review your case efficiently and reduces the chances of misinterpretation or oversight.

**Privacy Considerations**: Be mindful of privacy laws when sharing medical information. Only provide records relevant to the injuries from the accident.

## Handling Disputes Over Medical Claims

**Adjuster Tactics**: Recognize that adjusters may attempt to downplay the severity of your injuries or argue that they are unrelated to the accident. Be prepared to counter such tactics with evidence and professional medical opinions.

**Seek Expert Opinion**: In cases of dispute, consider obtaining an independent medical examination (IME) from a trusted healthcare professional to provide an objective opinion on your injuries.

**Legal Assistance**: If disputes over medical claims persist, consulting with a personal injury attorney can provide leverage. They bring expertise in negotiating with insurance companies and can navigate the complexities of insurance law.

**Document your Correspondence**: Keep a record of all communications with the insurance company, including emails, calls, and letters. This documentation can prove helpful in case of further disputes or legal proceedings.

Overall, dealing with insurance adjusters and handling medical claims requires a strategic and well-documented approach. By understanding the tactics used by insurance companies and preparing accordingly, you can enhance your chances of a fair settlement. Remember, in cases of significant disputes, having legal counsel on your side can be an indispensable resource for protecting your interests.

The importance of addressing medical issues with utmost seriousness following an auto accident cannot be overstated. Prioritize your health and well-being and recognize the crucial role comprehensive medical documentation plays in navigating insurance and legal procedures. Your diligent attention to these aspects can ensure a holistic recovery and fair handling of your case.

## Chapter 4: Managing Injuries and Medical Issues - Summary Checklist

**Common Auto Accident Injuries**:

- ☐ Familiarize yourself with common injuries like whiplash, fractures, head injuries, and soft tissue damage.
- ☐ Be aware of symptoms and seek immediate medical evaluation, even for minor injuries.

**Tracking Your Medical Treatment, Records, and Expenses**:

- ☐ Keep detailed records of all medical treatments, including dates of visits, types of treatments, and progress notes.
- ☐ Organize and safely store all medical documents, including prescriptions, diagnoses, and treatment plans.

**Understanding and Dealing with Trauma**:

- ☐ Recognize the psychological impact of auto accidents, such as PTSD, anxiety, or depression. Seek professional mental health support if you're experiencing emotional or psychological distress.
- ☐ Document any mental health treatments or counseling sessions for future reference.

**Long-term Health Consequences**:

- ☐ Understand the potential for long-term or permanent health issues resulting from auto accident injuries.
- ☐ Plan for possible life adjustments, including changes in lifestyle or work capacity due to chronic pain or disabilities.

Effective management of medical issues and injuries post-auto accident is crucial for both your physical and mental recovery. Staying informed about common injuries, being vigilant about long-term health implications, meticulously tracking medical treatment, and addressing psychological trauma are all integral parts of navigating the recovery process. Remember, your proactive approach in these areas not only aids in your healing but also fortifies your position in any related insurance or legal matters.

---

Don't miss out on our essential checklists! Click the QR code or visit https://www.pinderplotkin.com/crash-course-checklist to get your copy and stay prepared at every step of your auto accident journey.

# 5. THE FINANCIAL IMPLICATIONS

The aftermath of an auto accident often involves significant financial implications. So, we wrote this chapter to guide you through the various financial aspects, including managing medical bills, understanding insurance coverages, and exploring compensation avenues for your losses and damages.

## Handling Medical Bills

Dealing with medical bills after an auto accident involves navigating a complex array of costs. The financial burden can be substantial, from the initial emergency care to the potential long-term treatments and rehabilitation.

### Immediate and Ongoing Medical Costs

The medical expenses following an auto accident can vary greatly. Immediate costs often include emergency room fees, facility bills, diagnostic tests, and initial treatment costs. The cost can quickly escalate if long-term care, such as surgeries, specialized therapies, or ongoing medication, becomes necessary. For severe injuries, there might also be costs associated with rehabilitation, physical therapy, or mental health counseling.

### Strategies for Managing Medical Expenses

**Review and Negotiate Bills**: Carefully review all medical bills for accuracy. Don't hesitate to negotiate with healthcare providers for reduced charges or payment terms, especially if uninsured or underinsured.

**Payment Plans**: Many hospitals and clinics offer payment plans that allow you to pay off bills over time. These can help manage large expenses without incurring significant financial strain.

**Financial Assistance Programs**: Explore financial assistance programs that may be available. Many hospitals have charity care programs for those who qualify, and there are governmental and nonprofit programs that offer aid for medical expenses.

**Insurance Claims**: Ensure all medical costs are accurately documented and submitted to your insurance company. If the accident was due to someone else's negligence, you could recover these costs through an insurance claim or legal settlement.

Managing medical expenses post-auto accidents requires a proactive approach. Familiarizing yourself with the range of costs and exploring available options for negotiation and assistance are necessary to mitigate the financial impact of your medical care. Remember, keeping detailed records of all expenses is crucial for insurance claims and potential legal action.

## Understand Your Insurance Coverage

Navigating your insurance policy after an auto accident is crucial for clearly understanding your coverage and rights. Familiarizing yourself with standard insurance terms can significantly aid. In comparison, navigating the insurance policy's coverage and your rights. You should have a clear understanding of these aspects of your policy:

**Liability Coverage**: This covers damages or injuries you may cause to others in an accident.

**Collision Coverage**: It pays for damages to your vehicle resulting from a collision, regardless of fault.

**Comprehensive Coverage**: This covers non-collision-related damages to your vehicle, such as those from theft or natural disasters.

**Personal Injury Protection (PIP)**: PIP covers medical expenses for you and your passengers, regardless of who is at fault.

## Working with Your Insurance Company

**Clear Communication**: When reporting the accident to your insurer, provide clear and factual information. Avoid admitting fault or speculating about the accident's causes.

**Filing a Claim**: Submit all necessary documentation promptly. This includes police reports, medical records, and evidence of expenses.

**Handling Claim Denials**: If your claim is denied, request a detailed explanation from the insurer. Review your policy to understand the decision, and if necessary, consider appealing the denial or seeking legal advice.

By understanding the specifics of your policy and maintaining clear communication with your insurer, you can get the most out of your insurance coverage. Being proactive and informed can streamline the claims process and help ensure you receive the coverage you're entitled to.

## Lost Wages and Employment Implications

An auto accident's impact often extends into the realm of financial stability, mainly through lost wages. This effect can compound the stress of recovery, making understanding and documenting these losses crucial for your financial health.

### Calculating Lost Wages

**Gather Evidence**: Start by collecting documentation of your earnings. For employed individuals, this includes recent pay stubs or a letter from your employer detailing your average wages. For the self-employed, income documentation can come from bank statements, client invoices, and tax returns from the previous year.

**Determine the Amount**: Calculate your lost wages by considering the hours or days of work missed due to the accident. Include all forms of income, such as salary, missed overtime, bonuses, and other financial benefits.

**Self-Employed Considerations**: Calculating lost income can be more complex for self-employed people. Consider the average income you generate over a similar period and account for lost business opportunities or contracts canceled or postponed due to injuries. Uber and Lyft drivers should immediately capture detailed weekly pay ledgers if they lose access. Even ledgers showing zero dollars earned are important. The more, the better! You want to provide at least four months before the accident by returning to normal work hours.

**Projected Earnings**: If your injuries impact your ability to return to work or diminish future earning capacity, I advise you to seek the help of financial experts or legal professionals to calculate projected loss of earnings.

**Employment Benefits and Disability Claims:**

**Employment Benefits**: Explore any available employment benefits. This could include using accumulated sick leave, paid time off, or other relevant company policies. Understand the nuances of your employment contract regarding leave for medical reasons.

**Short-Term and Long-Term Disability Insurance**: If you have disability insurance policies, either through your employer or a private plan, understand the process of filing a claim. These policies can provide a percentage of your income during your recovery period. They typically maintain the right to be repaid after your case if there is a financial recovery.

**Documentation for Claims**: Ensure you have thorough documentation when filing for disability claims. This often requires medical records that clearly outline the extent of your injuries and the expected time away from work.

**Legal and Financial Guidance**: Calculating and claiming lost wages can become complex, uncommonly, when projecting long-term income loss or dealing with uncooperative insurance companies. In such cases, assistance from financial advisors or legal professionals can be a valuable asset. They can help you navigate the intricacies of insurance claims and employment laws to ensure that you are adequately compensated.

Losing income due to an auto accident exacerbates an already stressful situation. It's essential that you accurately document and calculate lost wages for the sake of financial recovery. It's about recouping immediate losses and ensuring long-term financial implications are accounted for. Taking a thorough and informed approach to this aspect of your post-accident journey will increase your chances of securing the compensation you need to support your recovery and safeguard your financial future.

### Pursuing Compensation for Damages

In the aftermath of an auto accident, understanding the types of damages you're entitled to claim is essential for ensuring you receive fair and adequate compensation to aid in your recovery processes. You can encounter the following types of damage:

**Property Damage**: This includes compensation for damage to your vehicle and any personal belongings in the car at the time of the accident. It covers the cost of repairs or, in cases of total loss, the vehicle's current market value.

**Medical Expenses**: This pertains to all costs associated with medical treatment resulting from the accident. It covers everything from emergency room bills to expenses for ongoing treatments, medications, and rehabilitation services.

**Lost Wages**: If the injuries sustained in the accident have caused you to miss work, you can claim compensation for lost income. This includes not only the salary or wages lost but also lost opportunities for overtime, bonuses, or promotions.

**Pain and Suffering**: Unlike tangible economic losses, pain and suffering encompass the physical pain and emotional distress endured due to the accident. Calculating these non-economic damages can be complex, as they are subjective and vary significantly from case to case.

### Filing a Personal Injury Claim

**Initiate the Claim**: The process begins with filing a claim against the at-fault party's insurance company. You will submit a detailed account of the accident, supported by evidence like police reports, medical records, and witness statements.

**The Role of an Attorney**: Including an attorney in this process can be highly beneficial while sorting through the complexities of a personal injury claim. They can help accurately value your claim, negotiate with insurance adjusters, and ensure all legal procedures are followed correctly. The attorney will identify insurance coverage and evaluate the need for an asset search on the defendant(s) and any potential caps on damages. Note: some states limit the non-economic damages, such as pain and suffering, that a victim can obtain. Sounds harsh, right? It is!

**Determine a Fair Settlement**: A fair settlement should comprehensively cover all your incurred and anticipated losses. Your attorney will negotiate with the insurance company to reach a settlement that truly reflects the extent of your damages and suffering.

**Legal Proceedings**: If you cannot reach a fair settlement through negotiations, your attorney may recommend taking the case to court to seek adequate compensation.

Pursuing compensation for damages after an auto accident involves a thorough understanding of the various types of damages and a well-planned strategy for claiming them. An experienced attorney on your side can provide you with invaluable assistance and ensure that you receive a settlement that fully addresses the accident's impact on your life. Remember, the goal of compensation is not just to reimburse expenses but also to acknowledge and address the broader consequences of the accident on your well-being.

### The Role of Legal Representation in Financial Recovery

In the quest for financial recovery following an auto accident, the role of a personal injury attorney can be pivotal for the outcome of the case. Legal representation brings numerous advantages to the table, especially in maximizing your financial recovery from the accident. The most important of those being:

**Valuation Expertise**: Personal injury attorneys are adept at accurately valuing claims. They consider immediate and long-term expenses, including ongoing medical care, rehabilitation, and lost future earnings.

**Negotiation Skills**: Attorneys possess the negotiation skills necessary to deal with insurance companies. They are experienced in countering lowball offers and can argue effectively for a settlement that reflects the extent of your damages and suffering.

**Experts in Legal Complexities**: An attorney understands the legal nuances of personal injury cases. They can navigate complex legal procedures and ensure your claim meets all statutory requirements.

**An Advocate on your side**: Having an attorney means having an advocate who prioritizes your interests. They provide a buffer between you and the insurance companies, allowing you to focus on recovery.

### Attorney Fees and Costs

Personal injury cases commonly operate on a contingency fee basis. This means the attorney's fee is contingent upon the successful resolution of your case, typically calculated as a percentage of the settlement or award. This arrangement is beneficial as it provides access to legal representation without upfront costs. It also aligns the attorney's interests with your own, as their compensation depends on securing the best possible outcome for you.

An experienced personal injury attorney can ease the burden of navigating the claim process and significantly enhance your chances of receiving a fair and comprehensive settlement. Understanding the value of legal representation can be crucial in your journey to financial recovery post-accident.

### Dealing with Property Damage

Property damage following a car accident requires a series of steps to ensure fair compensation and adequate repairs. Proper assessment and documentation are essential to streamlining this process.

## Assessing and Documenting Vehicle Damage

**Immediate Documentation**: As soon as possible after the accident, take photographs of your vehicle from various angles to document the extent of the damage as soon (and as safely) as possible. Include close-ups of specific damaged areas.

**Professional Appraisal**: Have your vehicle assessed by a professional to obtain an accurate estimate of repair costs. This appraisal should detail both visible and potential internal damage.

**Keep Records**: Store all documentation related to vehicle damage, including the appraisal, photographs, and any reports from the accident scene. These records are necessary for insurance claims.

## Insurance Claims for Property Damage

**Filing a Claim**: Contact your insurance company for a property damage claim. Provide them with all collected documentation and the professional appraisal.

**Detailed Communication**: When describing the damage to your insurance adjuster, be detailed and precise. Ensure they understand the full extent of the damage.

**Negotiation**: Be prepared to negotiate with the insurance adjuster. They may offer a settlement that doesn't cover the full repair costs. Use your documentation and appraisal as leverage to argue for a fair settlement.

**Seek Assistance**: If negotiations reach a standstill or if the offer is significantly lower than your appraisal, consider seeking legal assistance from an attorney who can help negotiate with insurance companies more effectively.

Handling property damage claims requires a careful and documented approach to ensure that you receive adequate compensation to cover all repair costs. Taking these steps can help streamline the claims process and protect your interests.

## Chapter 5: The Financial Implications - Summary Checklist

**Handling Medical Bills**:

- ☐ Review and understand your immediate and ongoing medical expenses.
- ☐ Keep all medical bills and receipts organized.
- ☐ Explore payment plans, financial assistance, and insurance coverage options.

**Understand your Insurance Coverage**:

- ☐ Familiarize yourself with your insurance policy's terms, including liability, collision, comprehensive, and PIP coverage.
- ☐ Communicate effectively with your insurance provider and understand the process for filing claims.

**Lost Wages and Employment Implications**:

- ☐ Calculate and document any lost income due to the accident.
- ☐ Explore employment benefits and understand your options for short-term and long-term disability claims.

**Pursuing Compensation for Damages**:

- ☐ Identify the types of damages you can claim, including property damage, medical expenses, lost wages, and pain and suffering.
- ☐ Understand the process for filing a personal injury claim and the factors contributing to a fair settlement.

**The Role of Legal Representation in Financial Recovery**:

- ☐ Recognize the benefits of hiring a personal injury attorney.
- ☐ Understand the common fee structures for legal representation, such as contingency fees.

**Dealing with Property Damage**:

- ☐ Conduct a thorough assessment and documentation of vehicle damage.

☐ File a property damage claim and prepare for negotiations with insurance adjusters.

The financial aftermath of an auto accident can be devastating. Implementing a comprehensive approach, from managing medical bills and insurance coverage to dealing with lost wages and property damage. Understanding these various components and staying organized is the best way to ensure you are adequately compensated for all damages and losses. Remember, seeking professional advice where necessary can facilitate a smoother and more effective financial recovery process.

---

Don't miss out on our essential checklists! Click the QR code or visit https://www.pinderplotkin.com/crash-course-checklist to get your copy and stay prepared at every step of your auto accident journey.

# 6. HIRING A PERSONAL INJURY ATTORNEY

More often than not, navigating the aftermath of an auto accident requires legal expertise, especially when facing insurance disputes, substantial financial losses, or serious injuries. We've dedicated this chapter to helping you understand when and why you should hire a personal injury attorney and how to find the right one for your case.

## Choosing the Right Attorney

The relationship between an attorney and client is a cornerstone of any legal proceeding, especially in the context of an auto accident case. This relationship is anchored in clear communication, mutual trust, and effective collaboration.

## Communication and Expectations

Clear and consistent communication forms the bedrock of the attorney-client relationship. Clients must be informed about their case's progress, understand the legal strategies being employed, and receive regular updates on any developments. You should feel comfortable asking questions and expressing concerns and be confident with the approach and decisions being made in your case.

Attorneys are expected to be transparent, responsive, and patient in explaining legal complexities in layman's terms, ensuring clients are always in the loop and confident in the trajectory of their cases. Be aware of this and use it as a standard when interviewing attorneys.

## Trust and Collaboration

Trust is a fundamental aspect of this relationship. Clients must trust that their attorney is acting in their best interest, using their expertise to guide the case toward a positive outcome. This trust is built through honest interactions, ethical conduct, and demonstrated competence.

Collaboration is equally important. The attorney-client relationship is a partnership, with each party playing a crucial role. While attorneys provide legal expertise, clients offer valuable insights into their cases. Active participation and honest feedback from the client can significantly enhance the effectiveness of the attorney's work.

In short, a successful attorney-client relationship is characterized by clear communication, trust, and collaborative effort. This relationship is indispensable for achieving the best possible outcome in your auto accident case.

## Preparing Your Case

Successfully navigating the legal aftermath of an auto accident involves meticulous preparation and organization, particularly in gathering essential documentation and understanding your role in the legal process. This preparation is key to building a robust case and achieving a favorable outcome. The following are the documents you should gather for your attorney:

**Medical Records**: These are paramount. Gather all records of your treatment post-accident, including emergency room visits, doctor's appointments, diagnoses, treatment plans, prescriptions, and bills. These documents prove the extent of your injuries and link them directly to the accident.

**Accident Reports**: Obtain a copy of the police report, as it provides an official account of the accident's circumstances. If there are discrepancies in the report, note them down and discuss them with your attorney.

**Body-Worn Camera Footage**: In instances where police officers respond to the accident scene, request any body-worn camera footage. This footage can provide an unaltered perspective of the accident scene, interactions, and statements made immediately post-accident, adding another layer of evidence to your case.

**Insurance Correspondence**: Keep records of all communications with your insurance company, including claim submissions, responses, and settlement offers. This paperwork will help your attorney understand the stance and tactics of the insurance company.

**Photographic Evidence**: Include photos of the accident, injuries, and property damage. These visuals can be powerful in proving the extent of the accident and the damages.

**Witness Statements**: If possible, gather statements or contact information of witnesses. Their accounts can provide independent perspectives on the accident.

**Financial Records**: Document any financial losses incurred due to the accident, such as lost wages, medical expenses, and costs related to car repairs or rentals.

**Asset Searches of Defendants**: In cases where you might be seeking compensation beyond insurance payouts, conducting asset searches of the defendant can be instructive. This helps understand the defendant's ability to pay when substantial damages are sought.

**Medical Experts**: Enlist medical experts who can provide authoritative testimony on your injuries and treatment needs. Their expert opinions can significantly strengthen your case, particularly when there's dispute or ambiguity about the long-term impact of your injuries.

### Your Role in the Legal Process

**Provide Information**: Your primary role is to provide detailed, accurate information about the accident and its aftermath. Be transparent with your attorney; minor details can have significant legal implications.

**Communication**: Maintain regular contact with your attorney. Inform them promptly of any new developments, such as changes in your medical condition or additional correspondence from insurance companies.

**Depositions**: You may be required to give a sworn, out-of-court oral testimony deposition. This is a critical part of the discovery process. Be honest and concise and follow your attorney's guidance during depositions.

**Court Appearances**: If your case goes to trial, your presence in court may be required. Your attorney will brief you on court protocols and effectively present yourself.

**Settlement Discussions**: You may be involved in settlement discussions. It's essential to understand the implications of accepting a settlement and to make an informed decision based on your attorney's advice.

**Document Management**: Continuously update and organize your documents and share them with your attorney. Efficient document management can expedite the legal process.

Preparing for your legal case after an auto accident requires diligent documentation and an active, informed role in the legal process. Your engagement and cooperation with your attorney are crucial in building a strong case. Remember, your contributions, from gathering comprehensive documentation to participating effectively in the legal process, are integral to the success of your case. With thorough preparation and a strong attorney-client collaboration, you position yourself for the best possible legal outcome.

## What to Expect in Settlement Negotiations

Settlement negotiations are a critical phase in resolving an auto accident claim, and understanding the dynamics of these discussions is key to achieving a favorable outcome.

### Understanding Settlement Dynamics

**Negotiation Process**: Settlement negotiations typically begin after the plaintiff (you) and your attorney present a demand letter outlining your claim to the defendant's insurance company. The insurer then responds, often with a lower amount, initiating a series of negotiations.

**Factors Influence The Outcome**: Several factors impact the negotiation process, including the clarity of fault in the accident, the severity of your injuries, the comprehensiveness of your documentation, and the insurance policy limits. This is where your attorney's skill in articulating your losses and negotiating plays a vital role.

**Insurer Tactics**: Be aware that insurance companies often start with lower offers, expecting negotiation. They may also use tactics like delaying negotiations or disputing claims to push for a lower settlement.

## Evaluating Settlement Offers

**Analyze with Your Attorney**: Evaluate each offer in consultation with your attorney. Consider whether the offer adequately covers your medical expenses, lost wages, pain and suffering, and any other damages.

**Long-Term Financial Needs**: Factor in future medical care or potential lasting impacts on your income. Verify that the settlement accounts for both current and future financial needs.

**Decision Making**: Making an informed decision on a settlement offer involves balancing the desire for quick resolution with the need for adequate compensation. Trust your attorney's advice, but remember the final decision is yours to make.

Understanding the nuances of settlement negotiations and carefully evaluating offers with your attorney are crucial steps toward securing a fair settlement. This process requires patience, clear communication, and a strategic approach to ensure that the settlement reflects the true extent of your damages and losses.

## Preparing for Trial

While most auto accident cases settle out of court, some proceed to trial. This typically happens if there's a dispute over fault or the settlement offers are insufficient. Trials involve a more complex and formal process, including presenting evidence to a judge or jury.

**Understand the Process**: Familiarize yourself with the trial procedure, timelines, and what each stage entails.

**Witness Testimony**: Be prepared to give testimony. Practice speaking clearly and truthfully about the accident and its impact on your life.

**Court Etiquette**: Learn about proper court behavior and dress code. Being respectful and composed in court is crucial.

**Managing Expectations**: Discuss with your attorney the possible outcomes and length of the trial. Preparing for potential scenarios helps manage expectations and reduces anxiety about the process.

Being ready for trial demands a comprehensive understanding of the legal process, readiness for personal involvement, and a mindset geared towards the unpredictability of trial outcomes.

The legal aftermath of an auto accident is complex and often daunting to those who don't know where to start or what to expect, underscoring the invaluable role of a skilled personal injury attorney. Such a legal expert will understand and manage the nuances of your case and will advocate for your rights and secure fair compensation. We implore you to choose an attorney whose experience aligns with your specific needs and circumstances and with whom you feel a sense of trust and compatibility. The right legal partnership can make a significant difference in the ease and success of your recovery journey, both legally and personally.

## Chapter 6: Hiring a Personal Injury Attorney - Summary Checklist

**Choosing the Right Attorney**:

- ☐ Research and select an attorney with experience in auto accident cases.
- ☐ Ensure the attorney is a good fit for your specific needs.
- ☐ Maintain clear and regular communication with your attorney.
- ☐ Understand your role in the legal process and collaborate effectively.

**Preparing Your Case**:

- ☐ Understand your insurance coverage and how to manage claims.
- ☐ Calculate and document lost wages and employment benefits.
- ☐ Explore options for disability claims if necessary.
- ☐ Understand the types of damages you can claim.
- ☐ Assess and document vehicle and property damage with a professional
- ☐ Navigate property damage claims with insurance adjusters.

**Your Role in the Legal Process**:

- ☐ Familiarize yourself with the legal process.
- ☐ Compile all necessary documents: medical records, police reports, insurance correspondence.
- ☐ Keep a detailed record of all accident-related expenses.

**What to Expect in Settlement Negotiations**:

- ☐ Review different settlement dynamics.
- ☐ Evaluate settlement offers.
- ☐ Learn the best way to make a decision.

**Preparing for Trial:**

- ☐ Understand why and when a case might go to trial.
- ☐ Prepare for trial proceedings, including witness testimony and court etiquette.

I hope you recognize the value of skilled legal representation. Choose an attorney who aligns with your needs and offers the best chance for a favorable outcome. Use this checklist as a guide to help you navigate the legal complexities following an auto accident. Each step ensures a thorough and effective approach to your legal journey.

---

Don't miss out on our essential checklists! Click the QR code or visit https://www.pinderplotkin.com/crash-course-checklist to get your copy and stay prepared at every step of your auto accident journey.

# 7. LITIGATION AND THE LEGAL PROCESS

It's imperative that all parties involved understand the legal process in personal injury cases, especially after an auto accident. This chapter aims to demystify the steps of a personal injury lawsuit, from the initial filing to the potential courtroom trial, providing you with a clear roadmap of what to expect and how to prepare.

## The Litigation Process

The litigation process of a personal injury lawsuit following an auto accident involves many stages and complexities. This journey typically begins with preparing and filing a lawsuit and progresses through several main phases.

### Overview of Personal Injury Litigation

**Preparation**: This initial stage involves gathering all pertinent evidence, including medical records, accident reports, and witness statements. It's where the groundwork is laid for the entire case.

**Filing**: The lawsuit starts with filing a complaint against the responsible parties. This document outlines your allegations and the damages you are seeking.

**Discovery**: Both sides exchange information through depositions, document requests, and interrogatories. This phase is crucial for building a strong argument.

**Pre-Trial Motions and Negotiations**: Motions and hearings are often before the trial. Simultaneously, both parties may negotiate a settlement, attempting to resolve the case without a trial.

**Trial**: If a settlement is not reached, the case proceeds to trial, where evidence is presented, and a judge or jury renders a verdict.

### The Significance of Filing a Lawsuit

Filing a lawsuit can be necessary when settlement negotiations stall or when the offered compensation does not adequately cover your damages. A lawsuit signals a readiness to escalate the matter to court, often bringing a new level of seriousness to the negotiations. It can be a strategic move to secure a more favorable settlement or, if necessary, to present your case in court for a fair judgment. Understanding when to transition from negotiation to litigation is a decision that should be made with careful consideration and legal guidance.

### Key Stages of a Lawsuit

Navigating a lawsuit in the aftermath of an auto accident involves several key steps, each integral to the progression of your case through the legal system. I organized them into 9 steps for you:

### 1. Filing the Complaint

**Draft the Complaint**: The first official step in a lawsuit is to draft the complaint. This legal document outlines your allegations against the defendant(s), the accident details, the injuries you suffered, and the compensation you seek. It must be constructed with precision, clearly stating the legal grounds for your claim.

**Submit it to the Court**: Once the complaint is prepared, it is filed with the appropriate court. This step initiates your lawsuit formally. The court reviews the complaint and assigns a case number, marking the official start of the legal proceedings.

### 2. Service of Process

**Notification of the Lawsuit**: After filing the complaint, the next crucial step is the 'service of process.' This is a legal procedure to inform the defendant(s) about the lawsuit and provide them with a copy of the complaint.

**Method of Delivery**: The service of process must be conducted according to legal standards, often involving delivery by a sheriff, process server, or sometimes via certified mail. It ensures that the defendant(s) are given fair notice and an opportunity to respond to the allegations.

**Proof of Service**: Once the service is completed, a 'proof of service' document confirming that the defendant(s) have been properly served is filed with the court. This document is crucial as it verifies that the legal requirement of notifying the defendant(s) has been fulfilled, allowing the lawsuit to proceed.

Understanding these initial stages – filing the complaint and ensuring proper service of process – is highly important. They lay the foundation for the legal proceedings to follow, setting the stage for pursuing justice and compensation in your auto accident case.

### 3. Discovery Phase

The discovery phase is the next component of the litigation process in a personal injury lawsuit, as it allows both parties to gather pertinent information and evidence from each other. This phase lays the groundwork for what will be presented in court, shaping the case's trajectory.

During discovery, both parties can request and exchange detailed information, including written interrogatories (questions that require written answers), requests for documents (such as medical records, accident reports, and police statements), and depositions.

Depositions are particularly significant as they involve witnesses or parties to the lawsuit giving sworn testimony outside of court, which is recorded and transcribed for later use in a trial.

### 4. Prepare for Depositions

**Understand the Process**: A deposition involves answering questions posed by the opposing attorney. It's a formal procedure, and your words can significantly impact your case.

**Preparation with Your Attorney**: Prepare thoroughly with your attorney before the deposition. Review the facts of the case, anticipate likely questions, and discuss strategies on how to respond.

**Conduct Oneself Properly**: It's important to remain calm and composed during the deposition. Always listen to the questions carefully and answer them honestly and succinctly. Avoid speculation; saying no is acceptable if you don't know or remember something.

**Review and Clarify**: Review the transcript and clarify any misstatements or errors after the deposition. This ensures the accuracy of your testimony.

The discovery phase, particularly depositions, requires careful preparation and a clear understanding of the process. It's a time to gather crucial evidence and establish the facts underpinning your case, making it a vital step toward achieving a favorable outcome in your lawsuit.

### 5. Pre-Trial Motions and Hearings

Pre-trial motions and hearings are the next stages in the litigation process. They can set the tone for how a lawsuit will proceed or even if it will go to trial at all.

Common pre-trial motions include motions to dismiss and motions for summary judgment. A motion to dismiss is filed when the defendant argues that even if all allegations are true, there is no legal basis for the lawsuit. On the other hand, a motion for summary judgment is filed when one party believes that the undisputed facts of the case support a ruling in their favor without the need for a trial. These motions can significantly impact the case by leading to its early resolution or shaping the issues that will be addressed at trial.

The judge may address these motions and other legal issues during pre-trial hearings. This is where arguments from both sides are presented, and the judge makes rulings on various legal matters, including the admissibility of evidence and the scope of the trial. These hearings can streamline the issues for trial, set schedules, and sometimes even lead to settlements.

Understanding the implications of pre-trial motions and actively participating in hearings are essential components of the legal process, offering opportunities to steer the direction of your case strategically.

### 6. Settlement Negotiations

In the landscape of personal injury lawsuits, particularly those stemming from auto accidents, settlement negotiations play a pivotal role. Most of these cases are resolved through settlements before reaching trial, highlighting this phase's crucial nature.

Settlements are agreements where the defendant or their insurance company offers a sum of money to the plaintiff in exchange for dropping the lawsuit. They are common in personal injury cases for several reasons:

**Risk Management**: Both parties avoid the uncertainties and risks associated with a trial. The outcome of a trial can be unpredictable, and both sides often prefer the control that a settlement offers.

**Cost-Effectiveness**: Trials can be expensive and time-consuming. Settlements can provide a more cost-effective solution for all parties involved.

**Privacy and Confidentiality**: Settlements can be kept private, whereas trials are public. Many plaintiffs and defendants prefer to handle the matter discreetly.

**Prompt Resolution**: Settlements often provide quicker financial relief for the plaintiff than the lengthy trial process.

## Strategies For Successful Settlement Negotiations

Effective settlement negotiations require a blend of skill, experience, and strategy. Your attorney plays a crucial role in this process. These include:

**Valuation of the Claim**: Your attorney will calculate a fair value for your claim based on your injuries, medical expenses, lost wages, and pain and suffering. This valuation guides the settlement negotiations.

**Negotiation Skills**: Experienced personal injury attorneys have honed their negotiation skills. They know how to present a strong case to the opposing side and counter lowball offers.

**Communication of Strengths and Weaknesses**: Your lawyer will communicate the strengths of your case and downplay its weaknesses. This includes highlighting compelling evidence and mitigating factors that might reduce the claim's value.

**Advocating for Your Best Interests**: Throughout the negotiations, your attorney advocates for your best interests, ensuring that the settlement reflects the full extent of your losses and injuries.

**Readiness for Trial**: A smart strategy is to prepare as if the case will go to trial. This preparation demonstrates to the opposing side that you are serious about your claim, often leading to better settlement offers.

Settlement negotiations in personal injury cases are complex and nuanced. The guidance and representation of an experienced attorney are invaluable to this process. A well-negotiated settlement can provide fair compensation for your injuries and losses, avoiding the uncertainties of trial.

### 7. Prepare for Trial

Heading into a personal injury case trial requires extensive and careful preparation. This involves thoroughly compiling and organizing all relevant evidence – medical records, photos from the accident scene, expert witness testimonies, and detailed accident reports. Preparing witness testimonies is equally crucial, often providing the backbone of the case's narrative.

For clients, active participation in the trial preparation is imperative. You will likely need to recount the accident's details and aftermath, providing a personal and impactful perspective on how the incident affected your life. This can occur during depositions and extend to testifying in court.

Your collaboration with your attorney during this preparation phase is vital. It's not just about recounting facts-it's about presenting your story in a compelling and coherent manner. Preparing for testimony, understanding the nuances of the legal process, and maintaining transparent and regular communication with your legal team are essential. Your input and responsiveness can profoundly influence the dynamics of the trial, playing a significant role in pursuing a just and favorable outcome.

## 8. The Trial

A trial in a personal injury case is structured with distinct stages, each critical to the case's outcome. It begins with opening statements, where both sides outline their version of events and what they intend to prove. This sets the stage for what the jury will hear and consider.

The next phase involves the presentation of evidence. This is where both sides bring forth their arguments, supported by witness testimonies, expert opinions, and tangible evidence like medical records and accident reports. Evidence is presented purposefully, shaping the jury's understanding and perception of the case.

Following the evidence presentation, closing arguments are made. Here, each side summarizes their case, highlighting key points and evidence to persuade the jury in their favor. This is the final opportunity to influence the jury before they begin deliberations.

Jury deliberation is the process of discussing the case privately and weighing the evidence and arguments presented to reach a verdict. The length of deliberation can vary, reflecting the case's complexity.

Once a verdict is reached, it is finally announced in court. The verdict encompasses the jury's decision on liability and, if applicable, the amount of damages to be awarded. The conclusion of the trial marks the end of a critical journey in seeking justice and compensation for personal injury.

## 9. Post-Trial

Following a trial, the possibility of an appeal, where either party can challenge the verdict if they believe legal errors impacted the trial's outcome, might take shape. This appeal process involves submitting a formal request to a higher court to review and possibly overturn the lower court's decision, focusing primarily on legal, not factual, disputes.

If you win your case, collecting the judgment becomes the next step. This process can vary in complexity, depending on the defendant's willingness and ability to pay. It may involve formal procedures to secure payment, such as garnishing wages or seizing assets, especially if the defendant is not forthcoming with the awarded compensation.

The legal journey after an auto accident can be a complex and lengthy process, underscoring the importance of understanding each step. From initiating a lawsuit to navigating trial and post-trial activities, having a skilled attorney by your side is invaluable. They provide expertise and guidance, ensuring your rights are protected and your case is presented effectively. Remember, while the legal process can be daunting, being well-prepared, informed, and having professional legal support makes a significant difference in achieving a favorable outcome. Practice patience and persistence as you navigate this challenging yet crucial journey toward justice and compensation.

## Chapter 7: Litigation and the Legal Process - Summary Checklist

**The Litigation Process**:

- ☐ Familiarize yourself with the stages of a personal injury lawsuit.
- ☐ Acknowledge the importance of each phase, from filing the complaint to attending hearings.

**Key Stages of a Lawsuit**:

- ☐ Ensure proper filing of the complaint.
- ☐ Understand the service of the process and its significance.

**Discovery Phase**:

- ☐ Prepare for the exchange of information, including depositions and document requests.
- ☐ Actively engage in the process with your attorney.

**Pre-Trial Motions and Hearings**:

- ☐ Learn about the common pretrial motions like motions to dismiss or for summary judgment.
- ☐ Attend necessary hearings, understanding their impact on your case.

**Settlement Negotiations**:

- ☐ Understand the role and benefits of settlements.
- ☐ Engage in strategic negotiation with the guidance of your attorney.

**Prepare for Trial**:

- ☐ Work closely with your attorney to gather and organize evidence.

Prepare for personal involvement, including testifying.

**The Trial**:

- ☐ Understand the trial process, from opening statements to jury deliberation.
- ☐ Be prepared for the presentation of evidence and closing arguments.

**Post-Trial**:

- ☐ Recognize the potential for appeals and understand the appeal process.
- ☐ Be aware of the procedures for collecting judgments.

**Final Thoughts**:

Acknowledge the complexity of the legal process and the importance of having skilled legal representation.
Stay informed and prepared throughout your legal journey.

This checklist is designed to provide a structured overview of the legal process in a personal injury case. It highlights the importance of each stage and your active role in collaboration with your attorney. Remember, a well-informed and prepared approach can significantly influence the outcome of your case.

---

Don't miss out on our essential checklists! Click the QR code or visit https://www.pinderplotkin.com/crash-course-checklist to get your copy and stay prepared at every step of your auto accident journey.

# 8. MY CLOSING ARGUMENTS

As we reach this book's "closing argument" – and no, that's not just a legal pun but a heartfelt send-off – let's reflect on the journey we've traversed. From the immediate chaos at the accident scene in Chapter 1 to the complexities of legal proceedings in Chapter 7, this guide has endeavored to equip you with the necessary tools and knowledge for navigating the aftermath of an auto accident. We began with the critical first steps after the accident, emphasizing safety, injury assessment, and the need for precise documentation. Then, we discussed the post-accident procedures, highlighting the importance of medical care and dealing with the often-overlooked financial repercussions.

Our next stop was the legal landscape of the accident. Here, we unpacked the nuances of fault, liability, and the vital role of police reports and legal representation. As we journeyed through managing medical issues and delved into the financial aspects, the importance of detailed record-keeping and understanding insurance intricacies became clear. The legal exploration covered in the last two chapters provided a deep dive into the litigation process, from choosing the right attorney to preparing for trial, each step underlining the value of skilled legal guidance.

So, as we close this book – or make our 'final argument,' if you will – remember. At the same time, the road to recovery post-auto accident can be intricate and demanding when you are armed with the right information and support, you are well-equipped to navigate it. Each chapter of this book has been a steppingstone in building your resilience and understanding, preparing you for the journey ahead. And while this may be the end of our bookish journey, it marks the beginning of your informed path through the aftermath of an auto accident. Every journey, like every good story, has twists and turns, but with the right guidebook in hand, you're never lost. Now, go forth and conquer your post-accident experience with confidence and maybe even a smile – after all, you've just aced your crash course in auto accident recovery!

## You've Heard My Story: **Now Share Yours**

Your story matters, and I would be honored to hear it.
Connect with me and let your voice be heard –

**https://www.pinderplotkin.com/crash-course**

Additionally, for a more personal touch, you can watch my story unfold – simply scan the QR code provided below. Your narratives and experiences are invaluable, and together, they weave a tapestry of resilience and learning. Share your story, join the conversation, and become a part of this ever-growing community.

Stay connected and informed – join our newsletter for the latest updates and insights - scan this QR code.

Need a consultation, let's discuss your story - scan this QR code.